No doubt about it, Peter Boone's life definitely raised the wattage on God's glory—this young man shined the Light of Jesus wherever he went, and with whomever he met. Our Joni and Friends' Family Retreats just won't be quite the same without Peter's participation. Just how significant was Peter's life of service? Well, the remarkable book you hold in your hands tells all about it. So start turning the page, and get inspired!

—Joni Eareckson Tada
Joni and Friends International Disability Center

The title, *He Made Us Better*, says it all. Peter's life can inspire us all to appreciate the happiness that can be achieved through the love of sports and the joy of life.

—Dick Vitale
TV Basketball Analyst

He Made Us Better is a terrific story. Peter Boone was a special person that I was fortunate to meet one evening after a speech I had given. Sharing that moment and later learning of all the obstacles he had overcome and the people he inspired along the way, truly touched my heart. I'm thankful others will be able to read and learn of his perseverance and the impact he had on everyone he encountered. This story should inspire all of us to open our hearts, trust our faith and believe!

—Brian Cardinal
Assistant Director, John Purdue Club

D1489856

Brady
Christmas
2016

HE MADE US BETTER

A Story of Faith, Family, Friends (and Football)

DARRELL BOONE

WESTBOW
PRESS®
A DIVISION OF THOMAS NELSON
& ZONDERVAN

WestBow Press books may be ordered through booksellers or by contacting:

WestBow Press
A Division of Thomas Nelson & Zondervan
1663 Liberty Drive
Bloomington, IN 47403
www.westbowpress.com
1 (866) 928-1240

ISBN: 978-1-5127-7876-2 (sc)
ISBN: 978-1-5127-7878-6 (hc)
ISBN: 978-1-5127-7877-9 (e)

Library of Congress Control Number: 2017903855

Print information available on the last page.

WestBow Press rev. date: 07/07/2017

To "Peter's Village"

It's been said that "It takes a village to raise a child." Peter had a "village"—a community of special people who God brought alongside him, his mother, me, and his brothers during our journey, with its many twists and turns, mountains and valleys. If you played a part in Peter's or our lives—whether great or small—this book is dedicated to you.

CONTENTS

PREFACE

For years, numerous people had told me that I should write a book about the amazing life of our middle son, Peter. Pete was born with a very serious birth defect that stacked the odds against him from day one. But almost from that day, he made sweet lemonade out of some pretty nasty lemons about as well as anyone I've ever known.

There was a part of me that badly wanted to write the book. But there was another part that was hesitant and reluctant, for a variety of reasons.

Then one day I was re-reading a devotion I had written for *The Upper Room* a few years earlier, in which I quoted 1 Peter 4:10: "Like good stewards of the manifold grace of God, serve one another with whatever gift each of you has received" (NRSV). Then for the "Thought for the Day," I'd closed with, "How am I helping others with what I've been given?"

Peter was born with many challenges, which in turn brought a truckload of additional challenges for my wife, Sandra, and me. But over the years, I truly came to appreciate Peter as a gift. And now I found myself convicted on two counts—first by scripture, then by my own words. So I knew that the time to write the book had come.

My purpose in writing this book is to share Peter with you, the reader, in the hopes that you can come to know him, love him, and enjoy him as Sandra and I did, and as most all of those who knew him did. And that you could also be encouraged, inspired and challenged to play whatever hand you've been dealt—no matter how difficult—with faith, joy, courage, perseverance, passion, thankfulness, fun, and laughter.

My other primary purpose was to celebrate God's faithfulness through those many individuals who came alongside us to walk with us in our journey, some—but by no means all—of whom are mentioned here. Without their help, we would never have survived. But besides that, they made the journey a lot more fun, and our lives are richer for their having walked with us.

As I contemplated the task before me, it seemed to me that the best way to tell Peter's story was by simply telling some of the stories that made Peter ... well, Peter. So that's what I did. It was hard work, but it was also a labor of love. There were times I cried, times I laughed, and times I did both at the same time. I intentionally didn't try to tell all the stories, lest this turn out like four volumes of *War and Peace*. I also tried to tell the stories as concisely as possible, for the same reason.

I've grouped the stories mostly by topic rather than strictly chronologically because, frankly, that seemed to me to be the best way to tell Peter's overall story. But some of the chapters encompass decades. So if there's a little bouncing back and forth, or overlap, please bear with me.

Just a note: In case you wonder at some point, everything in this book is true, and it happened just like I described it. I couldn't begin to make some of this stuff up!

And finally, thanks for your investment of time and dollars in reading this book. While I've been a freelance agricultural writer for years, this is my first venture as the author of a book. It's been quite a different process than writing magazine articles about corn, soybeans, and dairy cows. But I've loved doing it. I'm honored and humbled by your selecting it, and pray you'll be blessed in your reading of it.

Sincerely,

Darrell Boone

PROLOGUE

A Shining Moment

It was a pretty spring evening, May 28, 1994. My wife, Sandra, and I were seated, along with family and friends, in the crowded Southwood High School gym near Wabash, Indiana. Our son Peter was on the stage for the graduation ceremonies that evening, and as the evening unfolded, my mind flashed back over the past eighteen-plus years.

Honestly, I never thought he would get to this moment. Peter, our second of three sons, had been born with an especially severe case of a birth defect known as spina bifida, or open spine. When he was born, his prognosis had been very poor. Then it got worse. Over the span of his life, he had endured more than eighty surgeries—many of them "big league" caliber—and had been near death more times than we could count. Seven years earlier, during one of those surgeries, he had experienced trauma to his brainstem and had lost his ability to speak, swallow, eat normally, or survive without the benefit of oxygen during the day and a ventilator at night.

In previous years, children born with this defect usually didn't live long. But medical science had advanced to the point where Peter was one of the first generation of kids with spina bifida to make it into adulthood.

He had endured countless hospitalizations, several that were months in duration. He had spent most of the last semester of his senior year in Indianapolis's Riley Children's Hospital Intensive Care Unit, recovering from extensive skin grafting on his back for pressure sores that raged out of control, and would need further surgery soon.

But through bulldog determination, he had let nothing get in the way of being able to reach this moment, and graduate with his friends and classmates.

Despite what many would consider an incredibly difficult life, God had been faithful to him and us, and Peter had nevertheless turned into one of the happiest, most joyful, fun-loving individuals around. He was a popular member of his senior class and quite a social being.

A couple of Peter's endearing characteristics were a ready smile and being a "world-class laugher." He enjoyed life and enjoyed people, and was always ready for a good laugh at the slightest hint of a funny remark. St. Nick's round little belly may have "shook when he laughed like a bowl full of jelly," but when Peter really laughed, every single molecule of him laughed. When his laugh meter hit a "10," he'd clap his hands, and convulse forward in his wheelchair, and happy tears would run down his cheeks. And you didn't have to be a natural-born comedian to draw a good laugh from Peter. For someone to smile and laugh that easily just made people feel good and comfortable to be in his presence, and made them feel more like laughing themselves.

His sunny and outgoing disposition overshadowed his medically-loaded-down wheelchair in such a way as to make him come across to others as "really pretty normal." Countless people had told Sandra and me over the years that Peter's faith, courage, and determination had been such an inspiration to them. The message was almost invariably the same.

"Sometimes I think I've got problems. But I look at Peter with all he's been through, and see him being happy, enjoying life, and accomplishing his goals. Then I think if Peter can do that, maybe I need to quit feeling sorry for myself and try to approach things more like he does."

Peter wasn't on the stage—complete with wheelchair, oxygen tanks, suction machine, and other assorted medical devices—because he was the valedictorian, salutatorian, or had achieved anything else that would normally qualify as distinction. He was there because he'd requested to offer a simple prayer of thanks to God, and all those who God had brought into our lives, to help him on his amazing journey to this point. His request had been granted, and Mr. Conrad, the senior sponsor, would be reading his remarks for him soon.

As we sat there in the gym, I thought about how some of Peter's happiest experiences had taken place there. From the time he was a toddler, Peter had loved sports. One of the great ironies of his life was that while he couldn't play any of them himself, he had developed an incredible passion for sports that had been one of the hallmarks of his life and had given him a particular zest for living. And in his lifelong following of sports, he had taken legendary Notre Dame football coach Knute Rockne's axiom—"When the going gets tough, the tough get going"—to heart. At his core, he had internalized the incredibly tough mental attitude of athletes who just refuse to throw in the towel—period—no matter how difficult the going. Now that he, and the rest of us who had prayed, sweated, and toiled to help him get to this point were finally here, I couldn't have been prouder of him if he'd have been receiving Olympic gold.

For most kids, graduating from high school is a significant achievement. But Peter had had to claw his way up his personal Mount Everest to get here. I had no idea what the future would hold. In many ways, I couldn't imagine that he would live a whole lot longer. If it turned out that this was his finest hour, given his triumphs over incredible adversities, it would have been a successful life. Whatever the future, I was just unbelievably happy and proud for Peter to have achieved this moment. Peter had surprised us, over and over, for going on nineteen years.

But as we were to learn, Peter had more surprises up the sleeve of his silver graduate's gown.

This is Peter's story.

CHAPTER 1
OUR WORLD ROCKED

"Sergeant Boone, report to the orderly room," came the announcement from the loudspeaker early on Thursday, August 14, 1975.

I was in my tent barracks at Camp Grayling, Michigan, where I was a radio truck team leader. It was Thursday of our second week of National Guard summer camp. This was the call I'd been waiting for the past twelve days of the camp. I sprinted to the orderly room.

"Your wife's getting ready to have the baby," said First Sergeant Cunningham. "You're free to go." Then he added, smiling, "Take your time, son. Be careful. She can have that baby whether you're there or not." I nodded, thanked him for his advice, then ran back to the tent, hurriedly finished packing my duffle bag, jumped in my car, and headed down the highway for Marion General Hospital in Marion, Indiana.

But Sergeant Cunningham's words of caution were quickly disregarded. For our first son, Roger, who'd been born four years ago, I'd just been released earlier that day from active duty at Fort Lee, Virginia. I had wound up in the delivery room, in my dress greens, a scant two minutes before he arrived. I was determined that this time I *would* be there in time. As I raced down US 127 and I-69, the speedometer rarely dropped below ninety. Traffic was surprisingly light, and I didn't see a single policeman all 350 miles.

When I got to the hospital, around 11:30 a.m.—still in my combat boots and army fatigues—Sandra was in the delivery room and looked relaxed and happy that I'd made it in time. I quickly slipped on a gown, kissed her, and squeezed her hand as we were both relieved that this time I'd gotten away from Uncle Sam soon enough to really be there for the birth of our second child. Dr. Shah, her obstetrician, came through and said it should be about a half hour.

Sandra was past her due date by about a month at this point. The doctor had tried to induce her before I'd gone to camp, but after half a day of minimal results, he'd called it off. But this time, sure enough, in about a half hour, things started happening in earnest. As the baby made its appearance in the world, we learned that we had a second boy! Dr. Shah, who was not Sandra's primary OB doc, and whom I'd not met before, laid the baby on a table to the side, and I noticed a bloody spot on his back. The first time around with Roger, I'd learned that newborns don't come out looking like the Gerber baby, so I didn't think much about it, and figured they'd clean him up shortly. Then Dr. Shah began talking to us.

"There appears to be some kind of a wound on his back," he said calmly, adding, "Nurse, can you please get the pediatrician?" He continued to talk to us, very calmly, very professionally. I don't remember what he said, but clearly remember that it soon kicked in that something was drastically wrong. Army fatigues and combat boots or no, I started to feel like I was going to faint. But I was determined not to. Something bad had just happened, and I figured absolutely no one needed for the husband/father to be passing out on the delivery room floor. Dr. Shah reiterated, this time stronger, "Nurse, can you *please* get the pediatrician!"

As I watched the baby, something about him looked different. He was pretty purple from the delivery, and his head, face, and eyes looked a little out of the ordinary. The thought flashed through my mind, *Did we just have a baby boy, or a "thing"?* Just then, he looked over in my direction and started to whimper. A flood of emotion and compassion came over me, and I knew that whatever we'd just had, he had feelings, and in his own newborn way, he was reaching out to us.

A few minutes later, cleaned up, in a blanket and sleeping, he looked pretty much like a regular baby. As I took him in my arms for the first time, I said, "Hi, Pete, I'm your dad." Sandra chided me gently. She'd agreed on the name Peter, but was not overly fond of "Pete." But whatever we called him, he was ours, and we would love him.

Aftershock

Very soon, our pediatrician, Dr. Wojcik, did show up, and told us as gently as she could that they would be taking Peter by ambulance to Riley Hospital. The words "Riley Hospital" hit me like one of the tanks at Camp Grayling. I had heard of Riley Hospital, where in Indiana, it was for the most difficult cases of children. Now we had a son who was headed there.

I didn't go with him. I was in shell shock, as was Sandra, and I figured I needed to be with her, and we'd catch up with Peter later. Many times since, I've kicked myself for not going. But in my defense, I'd never done this before, and no one told me I needed to go.

At some point, I stepped out and told Sandra's mom, Beverly Overman, who was in the waiting room, what all had happened and was going on. I'm not sure what I expected from her, but it wasn't what I got. She seemed to have an incredible sense of peace, and just smiled gently, even as I dropped a bomb on her.

Then I returned to Sandra's hospital room. We talked for a while, cried for a while, and then I told her to rest. I stepped out for just a few minutes to try to take in what had just happened and get myself pulled together. I wasn't gone long, but as things turned out it was too long.

"They just called me from Riley," she sobbed uncontrollably. "This doctor told me that Peter had this birth defect called spina bifida, or open spine. He also said that Peter's defect was both high and large, which put two huge strikes against him. He told me that he would probably never walk, that he wouldn't be able to control his bladder or bowels, that he could be mentally impaired, and his life expectancy wasn't very long, and there could be a lot of other complications. The doctor said there was a good chance he might have to be institutionalized. Then he said, 'If we're going to treat him, we need to do surgery on his back right away. Do you want to give permission?' I didn't know what to say, but I told them yes. Do you think I told him the right thing? I wish you'd been here."

I wished I had too. I felt so bad for her, having to make a decision of that magnitude while all alone, having just delivered a baby with a serious birth defect, and in a state of total shock. I assured her that I'd have made the same decision. But in my own mind, had I been there, hearing what she heard, I'm honestly not sure what I would have said. I think I would have said the same thing, but hearing that kind of horrid news, in a state of total shock, I'm not totally sure what I would have done. But at that moment in time, I was okay with what she'd told the doctor.

Riley Hospital 101

For the first few days, Sandra and I were inconsolable. I was twenty-seven and she twenty-six, and neither of us had seen this coming. We felt like we'd been hit by a train, and our lives were in shambles. She was released from the hospital on Saturday morning. Bringing her home from the hospital where she'd just had a baby, with no new baby in tow, was the emptiest feelings either of us had ever experienced.

As soon as Sandra was able to travel that week, we went down to Indianapolis, about two hours to the south, to see Peter. We'd heard of Riley Hospital all of our lives. They dealt with the most difficult pediatric cases in the state there, and I was expecting some drab, depressing place filled with horribly sick kids. But what we experienced there was anything but that. It was bright and cheery, and the staffers were helpful and upbeat. Riley was named after James Whitcomb Riley, "the Hoosier Poet," who was fond of kids. One of his better-known poems was "The Raggedy Man," and each kid who was a patient received a Raggedy Ann or Andy doll, and the hospital was filled with them.

When we got to newborn ICU, we were required to scrub, gown, and glove up. When we saw Peter for the first time since that first day, he was sleeping peacefully in an incubator, even though he had originally weighed in at eight-plus pounds. As Sandra and I took turns holding him, rocking him, and talking with him, we felt much relieved, and Peter seemed to feel comfortable being held by us. We didn't know what the future held, but for now, we were enjoying spending time with our new son.

At the time, Sandra and I were working at White's Institute (later White's Residential and Family Services) near Wabash, Indiana, a large, Quaker-affiliated residential treatment center and school for troubled kids. I was a case manager, and she was the campus nurse, and we lived on campus with most of the other staff. White's was good about giving us time off to adjust to our new situation, and we made the trip to Riley frequently.

We learned that the doctor who had originally called Sandra was a resident, and he had come across as very cold and matter-of-fact. But when we met Peter's neurosurgeon, Dr. Henry Feuer, he was young, very caring, encouraging, and upbeat. We liked him immediately. He explained how he'd surgically closed the opening in Peter's back that first day, to get covering on the nerve endings that were exposed by the defect. He also told us that almost all children with spina bifida also have hydrocephalus, more commonly known as water on the brain, but that it could be managed well with the surgical implant of a shunt into the lower right side of the child's skull, behind the ear. The shunt and a tube would drain excess spinal fluid from the brain down the abdomen, where it would be eliminated. Peter had this surgery after about ten days.

We also met Dr. Richard Lindseth, an orthopedic doctor, who we also liked right away, and who was equally helpful in orthopedic matters. Before Peter was released from Riley after seventeen days, Dr. Lindseth showed us some range-of-motion exercises to keep his nonfunctioning legs from getting stiff and immobile. One of the things he said early on was that even though Peter would be somewhat fragile, not to treat him "like a China doll, but as much as possible like any other baby boy."

Over the next several months, we became very well acquainted with Riley Hospital, traveling there frequently for doctor appointments, clinics, etc. One of the clinic nurses, a lady named Betty Hight, was an "old pro," who was quite helpful to us. At one point she told us a little bit of her experience, which we really came to appreciate repeatedly. "One thing I've seen a lot over the years is that with a special child, God often gives them a little extra spark in their personality to help them compensate."

What's God Up To?

As we numbly groped our way through those first few days and weeks, our world had been rocked like nothing had ever rocked it before. We vacillated between feeling okay and upbeat, and depressed and inconsolable. We were comforted by many family and friends, many of them Christians. But one question that was front-and-center in our crisis was, "What's God's role in this mess?"

Sandra and I had both been Christians from our youth, but this new situation tested us like nothing ever had before. I clearly remember thinking, *If God's good and all powerful, then why did he let our son be born defective, with a lifetime of challenges in front of him? And what about Sandra and I? Doesn't he care what we're going through, and how bad we're hurting? Is God really good, or just some celestial jerk? Or does God even exist at all?*

On the other hand, at the same time, my every instinct was saying that all my life I'd been taught that God was good, loved us, and was always there for us. Although we were in the biggest turmoil of our lives, somehow deciding to suddenly turn our back on God didn't seem to make a whole lot of sense either.

I was always one to question things more than Sandra, and had something of a logical and skeptical nature. Ultimately, for me, it came down to a matter of we were in a mess, and for better or worse, we were going to need help like we'd never needed it before. And although I couldn't begin to make sense of what God was up to, I knew that we needed help. For me, realistically, God was the only game in town.

Although I'd come down on that side of the argument, it still took me years of searching and growing to gradually make a peace with many of my questions. But we also decided that, with God's help, we were going to try to make the best of our new situation.

Settling Into a New Reality

Where we worked at White's was a unique, rich, stimulating environment. At that time, most of the staff lived on campus, in campus housing, something similar to a pastoral/parsonage arrangement. The whole place had a real sense of family to it, where people—both students and staff—worked closely together, lived together on campus, our kids played together with other staff kids, and just about everyone ate together in the campus cafeteria.

As we adjusted to our new situation, we'd take Peter to the cafeteria with us for lunch, and set him on one of the cafeteria tables in his little adjustable carrier. He'd alternate between sleeping peacefully through the drone of cafeteria noise, and responding to the many people who'd come up to smile, talk, or otherwise interact with him. During this time in his life, he was much like any other staff infant who frequented the White's cafeteria.

"I can't believe what a good-natured baby he is," said Rich Davis, who was the assistant director at the time. "He's smiling and laughing all the time."

One of the things I remember from those early days was the staff going together to take up a "love offering" for us. Rich's wife, Sandy, gave us the proceeds, which was a generous amount. I really struggled with this at first. I remember thinking, *We can do this by ourselves; we don't need for other people to help us, to give us charity.* I was really kind of embarrassed, and felt very awkward about the whole thing. But it appeared that the only thing to do was to accept the gift graciously and say thank you.

Over the years, as Peter and we went through numerous crises, we were to receive many such love offerings, and individual gifts, some left in our mailbox anonymously. As much as I dreaded being the "helped," rather than the "helper," I gradually came to a realization that it was an expression of love, and that people really cared for us, were in our corner, hurt for us, and wanted to do something tangible to let us know those things. And the truth is we didn't have much money in those days, and with all of the out-of-pocket expenses that came with an infant with serious medical problems, we needed the help much more than I wanted to admit at the time.

Family Matters

I remember the night Peter was born, I had a tough time getting to sleep. I felt a heaviness come over me, the likes of which I've not felt before or since. What I realize now is that at that time, my body was sensing the full weight of what my heart and mind couldn't yet process. We were in for the challenge of our young lives, and had no idea where this thing was going.

As Peter was in his infancy, so too were the seeds of what we came to know as the "boy vs. burden" dilemma. On one hand, we'd early on made the decision not only to treat Peter, but to fully parent him as best we could. And from his earliest days, Peter was a delightful child. On the other hand, even as an infant, we immediately felt the burden of knowing that our future would be clouded with medical problems, the magnitude of which we had no idea of how it would impact us in years to come. This was coupled with the reality that, already, we were spending an inordinate amount of time and money on medical trips, occasional hospitalizations and surgeries, and other considerations. This "boy vs. burden" dilemma—the great kid vs. the heavy burden of his care, and the fact that the two were inseparably joined at the hip—was something we would wrestle with for years to come.

As we were to learn in those year to come, chronic illness with children takes a tremendous toll on marriages, with an extremely high divorce rate among those so impacted. We were just six years into our marriage; it had been great so far. But the coming of a child with serious disabilities began to take its toll and produce fractures in ways we would have never thought possible.

About a year into our new situation, we were desperate enough that we decided to seek counseling for both our marriage and for the burden portion of the equation that was Peter. The first counselor we met with was from a local agency, and neither of us felt great about him, but we were desperate, and thought we'd give it a try, which we did for a few months. But as we got into it further, he strongly urged us to consider institutionalizing Peter, for the sake of both our marriage and our mental health.

We never considered that. From the moment he first brought it up, there was nothing that sounded right about it, and the thought of putting Peter into an institution didn't compute at all. While that might have made sense for some other families, Sandra and I were committed to not only straightening out our marriage, but to also raising Peter—as normally as we could, for as long as we could—in our own home. Soon we decided to discontinue those counseling services.

Later, still desperate, we joined a counseling group through another agency. Then Sandra's mom had heard of a Christian counselor in Fort Wayne who had done some good work with some people she knew, so we started seeing him too. I knew as a counselor that seeing two different counseling services at the same time was not normal or recommended. But again, we were desperate.

While we did learn some things from the counseling group, the Christian counselor was the one who helped us the most. He found that Sandra and I processed having a child with serious disabilities very differently, and helped us work our way through that. But the thing he said that undoubtedly had the most impact on us was a question he posed to us.

"Do you want to have a child with a handicap, or be a handicapped family?" We'd never thought of it in those terms, but as soon as he'd asked the question, for both of us, it was a no-brainer. Having a child with disabilities was our reality. Being a disabled family was optional, and we wanted no part of it.

***

For the troubles we were going through, there was no miracle cure, no magic bullet, and no quick solution. But through our faith, counseling, the support of family, and bulldog determination on both of our parts to make things work, over a period of two or three years we gradually pulled ourselves out of the tailspin we were in. Very gradually, we experienced a healing in our relationship. And as time went on, and we faced numerous challenges together, and worked on Peter's care together, we drew closer, and our marriage became a really good one again. We were a good team. And we were so thankful we'd hung in there through the difficult times.

***

There was another time where we received some counseling services of a sort. At the time, White's had a couple of consulting psychologists from Ball State University, one of whom was a guy named Pete Mitchell. Pete was not only a good psychologist, but more importantly, a good guy who genuinely cared about people.

I'd worked enough with Pete that I'd got to know him pretty well, and we'd developed a good mutual respect. After Peter was born, he'd ask me fairly regularly how things were going, and I think that Pete, veteran clinician that he was, recognized earlier than I did that Sandra and I had a tiger by the tail with Peter. Sometime during the first year or so of Peter's life, he offered to do some counseling for us.

He came to our apartment on campus and did a few sessions for us. Still being not too far removed from Psychology 101, on one occasion I asked him, "With Roger, we've always encouraged him toward sports. From the time he was a baby, he always had little footballs in his crib, and we played catch, things like that. With Peter not having those abilities, should we encourage him more toward other things such as reading, or playing the piano, or something?"

Pete just smiled. "I think your best bet is just to relax and let your kids be themselves," he said. "They each have their own personality, and you and they are both better off to just let them develop their own natural interests."

CHAPTER 2
THE MAKING OF THE ULTIMATE SPORTS NUT

For a kid who was born with a number of serious disabilities, which became even more serious over the years, Peter nevertheless became one of the most passionate sports fans I've ever met. Here's how it happened. But before we get into that, I need to give you a little background on myself.

Growing up in basketball-crazed Indiana, I grew up dreaming of becoming a big-time basketball player. I started playing basketball in the fifth grade and continued into high school. I really wanted to play football too, and followed the Green Bay Packers faithfully. But my parents were farmers and thought that football was just some crazy sport that kids in the city played and got killed in the process.

After years of begging and pleading, they finally relented and allowed me to play football my junior year of high school. Having never played, I wasn't sure I could do it. But after three days of practice, I was playing first-string tight end, and immediately fell totally in love with the game. I even enjoyed two-a-day practices!

I experienced a reasonable amount of success in high school. But despite some encouragement from my coaches to play small college football, I never pursued it, a decision I later regretted. Instead, I decided to focus on studying engineering at Purdue University. I never became an engineer, but did get my undergrad degree in management from Purdue, where I became a loyal Boilermaker football fan.

A few years later, the opportunity to coach football was part of what led me to work at White's High School, where I served as an assistant coach for six years. Those were some of the best days of my life. But it was not to last. For financial reasons, White's dropped football after the 1978 season.

I never "got my fill" of football. It was a serious itch that never got completely scratched. For my entire adult life, I've loved football, have followed it closely, and, in 1997, became a Green Bay Packers stockholder. I was an "NFL owner."

For some unexplainable reason, all three of our sons (and now our grandsons) wound up having a real passion for football too, although it played out very differently in each of their lives.

Here's how it happened with Peter.

***

On the day Peter was born, Sandra and I were in a serious state of shock as we tried, unsuccessfully, to comprehend what had just happened. Shortly after he was born, our pediatrician, Dr. Wojcik, came in to tell us that because of the severity of his defect, they were going to immediately transport him from Marion to Riley Hospital for Children in Indianapolis. I remember her biting her lip as she hesitatingly and carefully told us the difficult news of the situation.

Crazy as it seems now, I almost asked her, "But will he be able to play football?" But this voice from my gut said, "Darrell, shut up! She'll think you're an idiot!" I've always been glad that I listened to that voice. But the truth is, as a dad who desperately wanted his sons to have that opportunity, that was what was on my mind at the moment.

Later, as a toddler, Peter wound up watching a lot of football. Every Saturday and Sunday, there was always a game on TV, and having very limited mobility, Peter wound up seeing a lot of them. I remember thinking that for a little kid, he really didn't seem to mind, and in fact genuinely seemed to be enjoying it. He also seemed to comprehend it, as much as a toddler can.

Learning to Talk—NFL Style

Having received a crash course in spina bifida by being instantly plunged into the middle of it, Sandra and I were acutely aware that being intellectually challenged was a possibility. Although we would have loved him regardless, we were nevertheless hopeful that he would not be disabled in both body and mind. But he was slow to start talking, and we were pretty concerned.

We were overjoyed when Pete finally started to talk a little, and did everything we could to help him pick up the pace. And football wound up playing a significant role in that process.

At the dinner table, Roger and I would frequently quiz Peter on football teams and mascots to develop his budding language skills.

I'd say "Washington," to which he'd answer, "Redskins." "Cleveland?" "Browns." "Dolphins?" "Miami." "Iowa?" "Hawkeyes." And so on, through an extensive roster of NFL and college teams.

He'd be excited and laugh when he was able to answer correctly, and really got into it. And I was surprised that, despite his heretofore reticence, he really had absorbed a whole lot more from watching football on TV than I would ever have imagined.

Obviously we worked on other aspects of talking too, but in his early days, that really helped to get the ball rolling.

And once the ball got rolling, it didn't stop for much. Peter loved to talk, and did it profusely. We called him "Chief Running Mouth."

Becoming a Boilermaker

From his earliest days, Peter very frequently was attired in some type of Purdue garb. Even as a baby, people would get a kick out of him having plastic pants with a picture of Purdue Pete or the Boilermaker Special on his backside. This attire, ironically, played no small role in his social development and personal identity.

That's because in Indiana, anyone wearing any kind of Purdue attire instantly becomes an irresistible target for Indiana University or Notre Dame fans. Or they receive a hearty affirmation from other Purdue Boilermakers.

Although we hadn't planned it that way, being a Purdue fan and regularly wearing "Old Gold and Black" opened countless doors that we could never have anticipated. Whether at church, school, doctor visits, hospital stays, or a hundred other situations, whenever people would see this little kid in a Purdue sweatshirt or cap, it would immediately draw a response, either kidding him or affirming him. For the people interacting with Peter, it gave them an easy avenue to begin a conversation. And to their surprise, Peter quickly ceased to be "an unfortunate little disabled kid," but rather one who would eagerly talk sports with authority and faithfully defend his beloved Boilermakers.

Peter was a born "people person." But being a Purdue fan played no small part in developing that to a much greater level throughout his entire life. Thank God for Purdue!

Coach's Assistant

When White's dropped football, I was suddenly an ex-coach.

About a year later, I attempted to get my coaching fix by becoming the coach for the boys' eighth-grade basketball team. I coached the Warriors during the 1979–80 and 1980–81 seasons. Neither team was very good in the won-loss column. But at White's, the expectations weren't high. Most of our games were with bigger schools, and kids who'd been playing together for years, and if you won a game a year, that was pretty much considered acceptable. Anything more was gravy.

While we didn't win many games, I did take a lot of satisfaction from the fact that our players—most of whom were some pretty squirrelly junior high boys and had never played anything except pickup games—learned their fundamentals, learned some sportsmanship, and both years made big strides in improving their skills, individually and as a team. More importantly, the kids had fun, and I was having a blast. My second year, when we won our first game just before Christmas, my team was so excited that they carried me off the court!

Roger, Peter, and even Philip (our third son, who'd been born in 1979) were regular attendees at our home games, attended practice when they could, and all became a significant part of the experience. Sometimes I'd take Roger and a friend to our away games, and occasionally I'd even take Peter. He was in a full body brace and walker at that time, and I'd just wedge him in between a bus seat for the trip. Then at the game, he'd stand out of bounds next to me on the bench.

The kids on both of my teams, but especially the second one, were great about helping Peter feel a part of things. At practice or a game, they would talk to him, give him high fives, pick him up and help him get places he couldn't go with his walker, and much more. Occasionally we'd have one or two of them down to our house, and they would spend hours playing basketball in our driveway or garage with Peter on a kid-sized goal.

"Shawn" was particularly close to Peter and Philip, and there was one time that Sandra had to take Peter to one of his doctor's appointments in Indianapolis, and the weather was pretty snowy. She was apprehensive about going, and I had something on that I absolutely couldn't go, so she took Shawn along to help her with the kids and just be along in case there was any trouble with the car in questionable weather.

Although likable, Shawn wasn't a model student. For many of the teachers and other staff, he was a serious pain in the neck. But he loved Peter and Philip, and couldn't have been a better helper on this occasion and others.

I never coached again after those two years. As badly as I hated to give it up, I was working on my master's degree in counseling at Ball State University, and something had to give. And although I fully intended to resume coaching when I finished my schooling, by then Roger was starting to play junior high sports. I wound up making the difficult decision that it was more important that I be a part of his experience than to continue coaching myself.

But coaching junior high basketball at White's was a great experience that helped Peter further solidify an athlete mentality and created a lot of good memories. For years after, Peter and I would laugh about something that happened during that era, and say, "Remember that time when …?"

Living Room Football

As our boys got a little older, a staple of life in our house was playing football in the living room. At the time, Roger would probably have been around twelve, Peter eight, and Philip four.

We had a regular routine. Roger would sit in a chair and play quarterback with a nerf football. Peter was stationed, sitting, playing "linebacker" down by the fireplace where the "goal line" was. I was in between, on my hands and knees as a defensive lineman

Roger would call a play and Philip would either run the ball or run a pass pattern. Usually we'd also have a pile of floor pillows in the middle of the floor, representing the line of scrimmage. Philip would frequently "dive over the line for a first down."

On a typical play, Philip would run the ball, and dive over the pile for a first down. Or he'd try to run around the "line of scrimmage," where I'd try to tackle him, but often would let him "break the tackle," and proceed on down toward Peter. Pete would manage to stop him short of the goal line about half the time, and Philip would break through for a touchdown the other half.

The boys loved playing football in the living room, and one of the most fun parts was an inadvertent part of our scrimmage. Invariably an errant nerf football would hit one of Sandra's potted plants, breaking off a stalk. I'd tell Roger to hurry up and just stick the broken stalk back in the plant.

A day or so later, Sandra would remark that "There's another stalk broke off of my plant. I wonder what's wrong with it?"

I'd just shrug my shoulders as if to say, "I'm not a plant guy; I really have no idea why it would do that."

The boys loved it! It became kind of an unspoken, secret, fun pact between the living room gridiron combatants that Mom wasn't going to find out the source of her plant's woes through any of us. And she never did find out, until all of the boys were well into adulthood.

Beating the Greek

As a Sunday ritual, after we'd get home from church, we'd immediately turn on a football pregame show. For several years, CBS featured "The NFL Today," with Brent Musburger and "Jimmy the Greek" Snyder, a Las Vegas odds maker. Musburger would ask the Greek his prognostications for the slate of games for that day, and Jimmy would give his prediction, including the final score.

I'm guessing Peter was ten or eleven at the time, and we were doing our usual Sunday post-church activity. After the Greek made his predictions, Peter just rolled his eyes and said, "Gimme a break; I could do better than that."

There was something about the way he said it that made me think that he was on to something. So I said, "Okay, Pete, what's your predictions?" He eagerly rose to the challenge and put his picks into writing.

We had to wait until after the Monday night game to get the final tally, but when we did, Peter absolutely blew the Greek away! It was no contest! Football is a notoriously difficult sport to predict, but Peter had easily whipped a veteran Las Vegas betting pro.

And really, it was no fluke. Very honestly it didn't surprise me that much, although I was amazed at how much better Pete did than Jimmy. He watched lots of sports on TV, would regularly devour *Sports Illustrated*, and I'd known for a long time that Peter "knew his stuff" and was something of a prodigy in the area of sports knowledge. But this took my level of respect for his feel for the game to a whole new level.

This incident marked something of a turning point for me. I began to realize that he wasn't just a kid who knew sports, but one who *really* knew them. He began to be my go-to source of information for all things sports related. This pattern continued for decades.

From this and similar experiences, I developed this philosophy in which I jokingly would say, "Never bet against Peter." And although that comment came out of a sports context, over the years, Peter dodged enough bullets with an assortment of near-miraculous survivals of various health crises that it came to apply to his "having more lives than a barn full of cats" too. His ability in both realms was amazing.

Conversation on a Toilet Seat

One thing I used to do with the boys every year at the start of football season to get us all fired up was to break out some video tapes, *NFL Crunch Time* and *NFL Crunch Course*. Both tapes contained classic footage from various Hall of Fame players' careers featuring outstanding hits, tackles, runs, catches, and more. Our favorites were of running back Walter "Sweetness" Payton, and defensive standouts Lawrence Taylor and Dick Butkus.

Butkus's footage was easily our overall favorite. For those too young to remember Dick Butkus of the Chicago Bears, he was arguably the best linebacker and most ferocious tackler to ever play the game. Even today, watching one of his videos is more than sufficient to get my competitive juices flowing, make me feel like putting on the pads again, and go knock somebody down.

One time when he was probably about junior high age, I was helping Peter go to the bathroom. As he was sitting there on the toilet seat, he said to me, "Dad, do you know what? If I could play football, I'd like to play quarterback on offense. And then on defense, I'd like to play middle linebacker, so I could stick 'em like Butkus."

His comment caught me off guard. On one hand I wasn't surprised, because that's kind of what I would have expected from him. I think what struck me was the way he said it—the conviction in his voice, and that there was no shred of self-pity in his comment. For a kid who had long since figured out that such things were never to be for him in this life, he nevertheless wasn't going to let disabilities get in the way of his joy in at least dreaming about what he'd like to do. For some time now he'd been living his dreams vicariously through watching classmates and players on TV. It was to become a lifelong pattern.

I was also struck by his passion for the game. Peter truly had what coaches referred to as the "killer instinct"—that very hungry, competitive, fire-in-the-belly, mentally tough will to dominate your opponent and decisively take him out of the game mentally and/or physically. Had Peter been able to play, I truly believe he was one of those types who would knock you out on the field, and then come check on you after the game.

That brief conversation on the toilet seat concisely confirmed what I'd suspected for some time. Peter had the heart and mentality of a warrior. And even though he couldn't actually play sports, through following them he still learned the values that they teach. As he battled serial physical adversities throughout his life, those never-say-die, when-the-going-gets-tough-the-tough-get-going, leave-it-all-on-the-field characteristics were not limited to sports.

***

And that's how it happened that a kid who had no ability whatsoever to compete in sports would instead turn his passion into becoming an All-American sports fan. And how God took my schoolboy passion and life experiences and used them to become a key part of Peter's personality. It opened doors to relationships that he eagerly entered into, in ways we never could have imagined.

I also think that at some point, psychologist Pete Mitchell's advice to two young parents—"Don't waste your time trying to 'mold' your kids. Just relax and let them be themselves"—kicked in. That was some of the best advice we ever received.

We did actually buy a cheap piano once, to at least try to give Peter an exposure to music. But it never went anywhere. He had absolutely no interest, couldn't carry a tune with a forklift, and with his lack of lower back strength, really couldn't sit on a piano bench well. Soon after, we sold the piano to Sandra's sister Brenda.

For most kids who play high school sports, those experiences and lessons learned become part of their identity. While Peter couldn't actually play sports, his passion for them became an integral part of who he was and gave him a lifelong interest. And throughout his life, it created natural avenues for him to joyfully engage with others around the topic of sports. Sports served him very well.

CHAPTER 3
"WALKING"

On the day Peter was born, we were told that the chances of his ever walking were slim and none. While some individuals with spina bifida are able to walk to varying degrees, the height and size of Peter's defect made it pretty much a foregone conclusion that for him, walking was "not on the table."

However, thanks to the efforts of Pete's orthopedic doctor, Dr. Richard Lindseth, all of us gave it our best shot. Here's the story.

Dr. Lindseth

We'd met Dr. Lindseth very early in Peter's initial hospitalization in Riley's newborn ICU. He was a tall man, fiftyish, of gentle disposition and a very common, easy-to-relate-to personality.

But this common-as-an-old-shoe demeanor belied his excellence as an orthopedic surgeon. A graduate of Harvard Medical School, we were to learn inadvertently that he had a national reputation in orthopedics.

One Sunday evening I was watching *60 Minutes*, and in one of the segments, there was Dr. Lindseth! I hurried and called Sandra and Peter to watch. He was there at Riley Hospital talking about using body bracing as a way to help kids who had challenges with walking. As the segment continued, it became obvious that our own Dr. Lindseth was a national authority on the subject, and as we were to learn later, was internationally known for his work in bracing and spina bifida.

But by the time we saw Dr. Lindseth on the *60 Minutes* segment, we were already well aware of body bracing for walking-challenged kids.

Body Bracing

I don't remember exactly how old Peter was when Dr. Lindseth first brought up the subject of "getting him on his feet," but he wasn't very old, maybe one or two. At first, Sandra and I were pretty surprised, given what we'd come to believe about his chances of ever walking.

But Dr. Lindseth just approached it matter-of-factly, saying that it was something Peter needed to do. He said we needed to do everything we could to give Peter at least something of an opportunity in that area.

The first step was what was known as a parapodium. It was really a pretty simple device—just a small platform, with two upright metal pieces and minimal leg bracing. About chest high was sort of a body wrap, in which Peter was secured with Velcro.

Simple as it was, it did "get Peter up on his feet." He used a basic little walker to be able to hold himself upright, and although he couldn't even talk yet, really seemed to enjoy being "vertical." It seemed to make it a little easier for him to interact with others. He really couldn't do anything that resembled "walking," but at least he could put weight on his feet and legs. We could also position him to be able to stand next to a small table or other piece of furniture to play with blocks, color, or whatever.

After a period of time in the parapodium, Dr. Lindseth said it was time to move up to the next step. This was a more sophisticated body brace, this time with no platform, which fit his body exactly. To make the device, we would spend hours in the Riley Orthotics Lab, where technicians would painstakingly measure, mold, and design Peter's next set of braces.

The next version was a full body brace that somewhat resembled an insect's tough outer exterior. The inside was lined with some softer material, but, again, he was secured by a chest-high wide strap, fastened with Velcro, as were his lower legs and thighs.

With this version, Pete moved up to a better walker that had wheels in the front. He also learned the "swing-through" gate. Essentially he would push his walker forward a few inches, then lift himself up on the walker handles and swing his stiffened body forward to a new position. Peter's shoes fit over the foot part of the braces and provided sufficient traction to keep him secure in these movements.

It took a little getting used to, but he enjoyed getting around on his own, and having a degree of independence from Sandra and me having to provide all of his mobility needs. Enough so that he learned quickly. Before long, he got much more adept and faster at it, and could get around the house easily. While it may have been at a turtle's pace by most standards, it was surprisingly quick for him, and enabled him to navigate at a reasonable speed.

In this brace, Peter attended Noah's Ark Preschool in Wabash at ages four and five, and really got along pretty well. He would stand for the entire time when he was there and was capable of doing most of their regular activities.

During this time, Peter was growing fairly quickly, and we soon moved up to the next version. Each new set of braces was a little more advanced than the previous one, and the new one had the capability of Peter's being able to either stand or sit. In addition to the insect-like exterior, the latest version also had a metal bar running up each side. The bar had hinges that allowed it to bend at both the knee and the hip, and was secured by a simple lock that could be moved up or down, depending on which position Peter wanted to assume.

And the longer Pete was in body braces, the quicker he got. With his walker, he could now move at about the speed of an adult walking slowly, but to see him go, it looked like he was almost flying across the room! And enjoying seeing how fast he could go! These were the braces that Peter had when he first started kindergarten, and he could easily "walk" from the van to the school door, then down the hall to his classroom. It was walking of a sort, but his hands, arms, and shoulders were actually doing most of the work.

When he was four, Peter was thrilled when Uncle Randy asked him to be the ring bearer in his wedding. Attired in a little silver tuxedo that matched the groom's, he took his duties very seriously as he moved down the aisle with his walker. He actually had to slow down from his normal speed to a more dignified, wedding-appropriate pace.

He got around enough that his walker really took quite a bit of use and abuse. We began to have problems with the frame breaking near one of the wheels. Sandra's dad tried to weld the break, even putting extra weld on the fracture, but to no avail; it broke again anyway.

We took it to Helfin Sheet Metal in Wabash to see if they could weld it and make it work. Mr. Helfin took one look at the walker, and asked Peter who'd tried to fix it.

"My grandpa," said Pete.

"What's he do for a living?" asked Mr. Helfin.

"He's a farmer."

With a twinkle in his eye, Mr. Helfin kneeled down to Peter's level. "Tell you what … I'll fix this for you on one condition. You tell your grandpa that he needs to stick to farming and let me do the welding. Okay?"

"Okay," said Peter, laughing.

I asked Mr. Helfin how much we owed him, but he wouldn't hear of it. The satisfaction of fixing a broken walker and having a bit of fun with a little kid named Peter, whom he'd never met before, was apparently enough payment for him.

Ominous Note

During those first several years, we'd frequently attend either national or regional spina bifida conferences when they were within a reasonable distance. Most of the time, Sandra's mom would pay our way to these trips as a way for the two of us to get a little time away, and learn the latest developments in working with disabilities. She would also stay with the boys, which she loved doing.

At one of these conferences, I believe it was in Ohio, one of the session presenters was none other than our own Dr. Lindseth! I've long since forgotten what his topic was, but will never forget one of his comments. He said something about kids with spina bifida getting along pretty well during their earlier years, but when they started to hit the growth spurt that accompanied their teen years, "all kinds of crazy things start to happen," which could complicate their care and management immeasurably.

At the time we heard that, I remember thinking that we were currently in one of those "tranquil periods" he was referring to. I also remember thinking, *That surely won't happen to us—I hope.*

From the time Peter first started in braces, we'd not ever expected that he'd be able to "walk" normally, but we'd also hoped that he would be able to maintain the option to either get around with a walker or use a wheelchair as needed. We really dreaded the idea of him someday becoming totally wheelchair-bound, seeing that as being "more disabled," or "less normal."

But as time passed, Dr. Lindseth's predictions began to come true. As Peter started to approach his teen years, "crazy things" did begin to happen. From the deformity in his spine, he began to develop scoliosis, which put more pressure on his skin against the braces. And as he moved up in grades at school, greater range was required for him to be able to move from classroom to classroom and beyond, which had begun to exceed his stamina.

Ultimately we had to leave the bracing behind, and Peter did move into the wheelchair full time. And while we hated for that to happen, by the time it did, we'd seen the writing on the wall long enough to know that it was inevitable, and that's the way it was going to have to be. His wheelchair was to become his constant and indispensable daytime companion. But he still seemed very "normal" to us and most people. After Peter would engage us or someone else in a conversation about sports or any other number of topics, we hardly even noticed the wheelchair.

***

Looking back on it, Sandra and I have no regrets about the years we spent trying to help Peter "walk." That's the way we tried to approach everything we did with Peter, to give him the best possibility we could with what we had to work with.

I'm not sure what Dr. Lindseth's goals for Peter really were. As a world-class orthopedic surgeon, he surely knew that walking was not going to be a long-term solution for Peter. My best guess is that he wanted to buy Peter all the time he could for his feet and legs to develop as normally as possible, and to help in some ways to improve his socialization and mobility.

While Peter wasn't "walking" for many years, when we look back on the photos from those days, Peter was clearly glad to have had that opportunity. Those were good times.

But On a Sweeter Note ...

After Peter was born, Sandra and I weren't sure whether we wanted to have any more children or not. We'd always thought we'd like to have three, but we had our hands full with Peter, and we certainly didn't need another child with serious medical challenges.

Then in early 1978 we were attending one of our area spina bifida meetings and were talking with another couple who had a child with spina bifida, and had made the decision to have another. The child was a fun little kid, and had been a good thing for their family. That got us to do some serious thinking.

Long story short, after going through some genetic counseling, much thought, and much prayer, it seemed the odds were good enough that we decided to have a third child. Philip was born on June 13, 1979, the fiftieth birthday for Sandra's dad. For all of our fears, he was a healthy, nine-plus-pound baby boy.

Philip turned out to be a very good thing for our family. It was also a lesson in how amazing it can be that three different boys, born of the same genetics, and raised in the same home, can be so different. Philip was an ornery little kid, who was into something *all* of the time. On any given week, he probably got into more trouble than Roger or Peter had in their lifetimes. But he was also funny, always saying or doing something to give people a good laugh. He became known—and not just in our house—as "Phil the Pill."

But Philip's was a "loveable kind of orneriness"—the kind that would earn him some time sitting in the corner for his consequences, and then Sandra and/or I would go into the next room and have a good laugh. And despite his many misadventures, he didn't have a malicious bone in his body.

Philip turned out to be a lot of fun, and very much filled a need in our family.

CHAPTER 4
SOUTHWOOD ELEMENTARY

Well before it was time for Peter to start school, we were scared. I'm sure just about all parents of children with disabilities have some apprehensions, but we were more than "normally apprehensive."

Soon after Peter was born, some friends from high school, who also had a daughter born with spina bifida, told us about a spina bifida parent group in Fort Wayne. We tried to attend some meetings when we could. At one meeting, the topic of discussion was children with spina bifida being excluded from regular classrooms, despite the passage of PL 94–142, the Education of All Handicapped Children Act, passed in 1975.

"Despite the law, there are a lot of teachers that don't want our kids in regular classrooms," said one parent, "and the principals are backing them." There seemed to be a general consensus in the meeting that this was a real problem.

Although Peter was still a few years away from school, we also knew that time would come before we knew it. As far as we knew at that point, Peter appeared to be of normal intelligence. He'd begun life with at least two strikes against him, had exceeded expectations so far, and the thought of him being excluded from regular classes was not remotely acceptable to us.

Although in some ways the scenarios that parents in the group had described seemed hard for us to imagine, it was obvious that they "weren't just making it up." So what were we to do?

As we pondered our options, at one point we even considered contacting the American Civil Liberties Union. As much as I disliked that organization and many of the causes they took up, I also knew that they would go to the wall to prosecute a case that infringed on someone's rights.

Meeting Mr. Arnold

Time did move quickly, and about two years before it was time for Peter to start kindergarten, we decided to at least find out where we stood in regard to Peter's being able to attend regular classes. We wanted to know early, in case we needed to fight for that right. So we scheduled a meeting with Bill Arnold, principal of Southwood Elementary, in southern Wabash County where we lived.

Before the meeting we thought, deliberated, prayed, and sought to figure out what would be the best way to approach the meeting. Finally, we decided to just go talk with him and see what he had to say. But as much as we really didn't want to start Peter's education off on an adversarial foot, given what we'd heard, I was prepared to push back if we got any resistance.

Mr. Arnold actually went to our church, but we'd never met him, we'd just seen him at a distance. When Sandra and I entered his office, we were pretty nervous. As he greeted us, Mr. Arnold seemed nice enough—a kindly, grandfatherly looking gentleman with a pleasant demeanor.

I started out doing most of the talking. I briefly explained Peter's history, medical situation, and such, told him that Peter was currently attending Noah's Ark Preschool and was getting along well, and as nearly as we could tell, seemed to be of normal intelligence. Then I popped the question.

"Mr. Arnold, will Peter's attending school here be a problem as far as his attending regular classes?"

He looked surprised that we'd even ask. Immediately he responded, "No, I really don't see why it would."

And it wasn't so much what he said as the way he said it. It was a totally sincere, straight-from-the-heart response. There was not a hint of him trying to be "politically correct," or "We knew this was bound to happen sometime," or anything like that. Just a good and caring human being responding with 100 percent sincerity to a couple of very scared young parents.

Immediately we felt a huge relief, a real peace, and felt very comfortable with Mr. Arnold. He reassured us that Southwood Elementary had a good staff, and that he was sure that any of the teachers would be glad to have a student like Peter in their classes.

Our discussion very quickly moved from my asking, "Will this be a problem?" to his asking, "How can we help?" Mr. Arnold asked us what Peter would need in the way of accessible accommodations, desk, restroom capabilities, etc. He thanked us for being proactive and coming in early to talk with him about Peter ahead of time. And he assured us that when the time came for Peter's first day of school, Southwood Elementary would be ready.

As we drove home, we felt a little bit foolish for having worried about it so much, or even considering anything but the approach we wound up taking. But our fears were real. It's impossible to put into words how relieved and thankful we were.

Making Friends with Teachers

We decided to start Peter in school a year later than we could have. His birthday was in August, which is fairly late in the year, plus he had enough challenges that we thought the extra year would help him.

When it was time for him to begin school, Southwood really was ready. A concrete ramp had been installed at the west end of the building, which we saw as a very tangible, welcoming sign.

Buoyed by Mr. Arnold's very encouraging gestures toward us,

Sandra and I wanted to do everything we could to make things work smoothly. A big part of that was getting to know all of Peter's teachers and other staff personally, and letting them know that we wanted to work with them to make their job as smooth as possible, and that we were available to help on very short notice as needed.

We wrote up a handout for any teachers, school nurse, and other staff who would be working with Peter, explaining his medical situation, care, and anything else we could think of that could be helpful to them. At the end, we gave contact information where they could reach us immediately if there were any problems. Fortunately we only lived about two miles from the school, so we could get there quickly in case of any difficulties.

At the time Peter started school, in 1981, I was working on my master's degree in counseling and had taken a course in IQ testing. Although Peter was too young at the time for the most-used children's test, I gave him the Peabody Picture Vocabulary Test, which was generally accepted as a good and reliable tool to measure the IQ of younger kids. Peter scored 118 on the test, which put him in the "bright" range, significantly above average (average is 100).

His assigned kindergarten teacher was Mrs. Jane Denny, who was one of the younger teachers on the staff. Shortly before school started, we took Peter down to meet her. She seemed to be a very caring person who, like Mr. Arnold, immediately put us at ease.

We introduced Peter, told a little about him, and gave her the handout. We also showed her about the locks on Peter's body braces, and how they worked for when he needed to sit down. Although the locks could be a little bit tricky at times, she figured it out quickly and seemed very willing to take the trouble to do it as needed.

We asked if she had any questions, and she seemed to have a good grasp of Peter's situation. We, including Peter, felt very comfortable with her, and if she had any apprehensions, she didn't show them. Again, we were very thankful.

True to his word, Mr. Arnold did everything he could to help us get off to a good start. One of the first items of business was getting a desk to fit Peter. At the time, he stood most of the time, and just used a motorized, scooter-type chair as needed. Mr. Arnold called a custodian down to make the needed adjustments. He made his best guess at it, and then asked Peter how it felt.

"Mr. custodian, could you make it just a little bit higher," Peter asked, showing about an inch with his fingers.

***

From day one, either Sandra, I, or someone else would run down to school at noon to help Peter go to the bathroom. Later we became familiar with a 1984 case on that very subject, Tatro v. the School Board of Irving, Texas. That case wound up going to the US Supreme Court, which said in a landmark decision that schools were required to provide that service for special-needs children.

While we knew our rights, we never pushed that one. Sandra wasn't working full time at the time, my schedule had some flexibility, and we were close by, so we just took care of it.

We could have "fought for our rights" and won, but our school corporation wasn't a big one, and likely couldn't have made that accommodation without adding staff. Very early on, we recognized that we had a good thing going; we were very appreciative, and didn't want to create any unnecessary burden. Why rock the boat?

First-Day Surprise

For any parents, their children's first day of school is one filled with mixed emotions. Peter's was especially poignant. We took him down to his first day and got him started in his class, with things seeming to go well. Kindergarten at that time was just a half day.

When we picked him up at the end of the day, Sandra and I couldn't wait to hear his account of how things had gone.

"So how did you like school, Peter?"

"It was great! I loved it!" he said.

"So what did you like best?" we asked.

"Gym class. I just love gym class!" he responded.

Gym class?

We asked him again, just to make sure our ears weren't deceiving us. They weren't. This was a little kindergarten kid, just starting school, who was in a body brace and walker, couldn't really walk or run, and he liked gym class the best of anything his first day of school? I knew Peter loved sports, but this caught me totally off guard.

"Yeah, it was really fun. I wish we could have it every day."

The PE teacher at Southwood Elementary, Felix Chambers, was actually my old high school football coach at Maconaquah High School in the next county. He'd been my government teacher, but since had become the coach of the Southwood High Knights, where he'd built a successful program.

It was a well-known fact that he used his elementary PE classes as his best recruiting tool. Any elementary munchkin who looked like he'd someday be able to run a good forty-yard dash or get big enough to open holes in the defense would be groomed for the next several years to become a football Knight.

Although we'd had our moments when I was in high school, Coach and I generally had a good relationship. I did have some concerns, though. I knew him well enough that he was definitely a coach first and not one to let his teaching get in the way of his coaching. He was also definitely old school, not all that far from retirement.

The emphasis at that time for kids with disabilities who were mainstreamed into regular classes was to receive "adaptive physical education," in which the teacher would work them into the regular class regimen while still targeting their individual needs. I was pretty sure Coach had probably never even heard of adaptive physical education, and not at all sure how open he'd be to my broaching the subject. I decided to just take a wait-and-see approach.

As with Mr. Arnold, my worries were for naught. At this point in time, I can't remember what all Coach did with Peter in gym class, but whatever it was, Peter loved it. Sometimes as part of the "PE curriculum" he'd teach the kids football pass patterns and have Peter throw passes from his scooter. One thing I clearly remember—Peter was strong, having built up his arms and shoulders from "walking."

With his body brace holding him perfectly straight, even as a little kid, he could do twenty-five picture-perfect pushups in a row, better than most high school athletes. Coach used to have Peter do pushup demonstrations for the class, which made Peter feel like pretty big stuff. At other times, it seemed like maybe Coach used Peter as a "cone," to mark the end of the playing field. Even as a lowly cone, Peter was thrilled just to be a part of things!

Although Coach Chambers undoubtedly never heard of adaptive physical education, he wound up working Peter into the class as best he could and making him feel an accepted part of things instinctively. And he did a marvelous job of it! As Sandra and I talked with Coach over the years, he told us how much he liked having Peter in his class. I understood much better why gym was Peter's favorite class.

***

Before long, we were picking up that Peter had a lot of friends at school, and was pretty popular, even from his early school years. One of his friends during those years was a little kid named Alex Falder. His family went to our church, and I'd seen Alex at little league baseball games, where Roger and Alex's brother, Mike, were on the same team. As a little kid at these games, Alex had struck me as kind of like "Taz," the Tasmanian devil in the Bugs Bunny cartoons, an endless ball of energy who went spinning from one misadventure to another for the whole seven innings. Alex seemed to get into more than his share of trouble at school. A few years later, Peter gave me an update on Alex.

"Alex really got into trouble today," Peter told me one day. "Mr. Chambers paddled him right there in gym class."

From my high school days, I knew that Coach's patience didn't come in unlimited quantities, and I wasn't overly surprised that Alex could get Coach to his last straw.

"What did he do?" I asked.

"We were standing in line waiting to go outside, and he gave the kid in front of him a wedgie," Peter giggled. "I thought it was kind of funny, but Mr. Chambers didn't."

Alex not only continued to get into more than his share of trouble, but even picked up the pace as years progressed, and started hanging out with the wrong crowd. After fifth grade, his mother transferred him to a Christian school in Marion to try to salvage him. More about Alex later.

Second Choice

When it neared the end of the first grade with Mrs. Livergood, Peter had his eye on what he hoped would be his second-grade teacher, Mrs. Schoeff. A young, outgoing, and popular teacher, Peter told me in later years that "Everyone wanted Mrs. Schoeff."

Instead of Mrs. Schoeff, Peter was assigned to Mrs. Carter. From what we knew of her, she seemed nice enough. But she was older, and Mrs. Schoeff already had struck up a good rapport with Peter, and we were pulling for her too. It just seemed that she might be a better match for Pete.

But we decided to stick with the original decision. Southwood Elementary was working great with Peter and us, and we also had confidence that if Mr. Arnold thought Mrs. Carter would be a good match, it would be okay.

Okay is a gross understatement. Sandy, as we came to know her later, was wonderful! Peter never had anything but good experiences with all of his teachers, but Sandy Carter was one of the best. She and her husband owned a beautiful neocolonial home just a short distance east of the school, and at the end of the year, she'd have her class down for a field trip/party in their scenic wooded backyard. Mrs. Carter always made special provisions to make sure that everything was not only accessible, but "just right in every way" for Peter on these occasions. She made the trip to visit him in the hospital in Indianapolis on more than one occasion, and at least one trip in bad weather. And much more.

She couldn't have been more caring for our son. "Second choice" turned out very, very well.

***

When Peter was going into the fourth grade, he was assigned to Susan Davis. Like with Sandy Carter, we really didn't know her, and were just hoping that she'd be a good match for Peter. As things turned out, she became one of Peter's all-time favorite teachers at Southwood Elementary.

Susan regularly went above and beyond to help her new pupil succeed. She spent extra time helping him with his homework. Once, when he'd been in the hospital, she spent a lot of time helping him with his science fair project. She visited him in the hospital multiple times. On one occasion, she alerted us that she'd noticed a deterioration in his handwriting and a change in his voice. This led to an eventual shunting of a cyst in his spinal cord, reducing pressure on his brain stem, and resolving the problem. Even after Peter was out of the fourth grade, she continued to be a special friend to Peter and us. Sometimes when Peter was in the hospital, she'd have Philip over to her house, to give some special attention. And much more that I can't even remember. She was as good a teacher and friend as Peter could have ever hoped for.

Homework Lite

Peter was a good student, and got good grades. One night Sandra had to go someplace, but before she left, made Peter and I promise that we'd work on his spelling words. She wouldn't leave till we promised.

Seemed to me she was a little over the top on this, but that's the way it worked between the two of us—she was more conscientious, I was less so. I very much believed in education but thought she got a little carried away at times.

So we started working on about fifty spelling words. He got about the first fifteen without so much as missing a letter. So I said to Peter, "Pete, I think you've got these pretty well. How about we stop here and work in a game of chess before bedtime."

He loved it, started laughing and clapping his hands, and we played chess.

"When Sandra got home, first question—Did you guys work on the spelling words?"

"Yep," I answered, without telling her we didn't slog through every single one. But Peter never could keep a straight face, and he started laughing, which tipped her off that something was up. She pressed it. I kept reassuring her that we had in fact "worked on the spelling words." She finally dropped it. But Peter and I had fun with our "secret" and many others like it for years to come.

Serious Meeting

In April 1987, Peter had the surgery that went south on him, losing his ability to talk, swallow, and eat normally, and that required him to be on oxygen 24/7, and a ventilator at night. He also had a tracheostomy, and had to use a suction machine for his secretions.

He missed the end of his fifth-grade year, and the first couple months of his sixth-grade year. Mr. Arnold and his teachers worked with us to keep him going academically.

But in October of his sixth-grade year, he was finally ready to return to regular school, but in a much different state. Peter still had his personality, but the part about not being able to talk especially worried us.

Before he returned, we arranged a meeting with the entire sixth grade. I talked and explained how Peter couldn't talk verbally any more, but he could mouth what he was trying to say, which worked marginally well. I also explained his other circumstances and asked for their patience, cooperation, and most of all, for them still to be Peter's friends.

You could have heard a pin drop. The kids were great. A few had some tears. But they listened and responded. For the rest of his time in elementary, junior high, and high school, Peter never spoke another word aloud. He either mouthed what he wanted to say, scribbled it on a piece of paper, or motioned messages with his hands. But they responded to the challenge. They included him. They were still his friends. And the teachers made the rest of it work.

After we got done with the talk, one of Peter's teachers, Mr. Brubaker, a fellow Purdue fan, shook hands with me. I told him I felt bad about the teachers having a situation where Pete couldn't talk. He just put his hand on my elbow and said, "Don't forget, we're flexible here."

We started out with half days, and Mr. Brubaker told us that Peter didn't need to come till nine thirty tomorrow because they had choir first thing. "I don't know what part Pete would sing anyway," he grinned.

Basketball Manager

Another of Peter's sixth-grade teachers, Dan Guenin, was also great with Peter. During the winter, Southwood had a basketball league for the elementary grades, and he asked Peter to be the "manager" for his team. Realistically Peter couldn't do much, but he was thrilled to death to finally be part of an athletic team. He mainly just sat next to Mr. Guenin during the games.

The one thing I remember from that season—in one game, Peter told Mr. Guenin, "These refs are terrible. You need to throw a chair, like Bobby Knight."*

***

Looking back, in those early days of PL 94–142, I'm sure there were problems in some school corporations with special-needs kids being accepted into regular classes. But for all our fears, we found absolutely none of that at Southwood Elementary, despite the fact that having a student like Peter was uncharted territory for all of them. All we found there was an administration and staff that welcomed Peter and us with open arms. They regularly went above and beyond to do whatever was needed to make things work. And who laughed with us and cried with us.

It's been nearly thirty-seven years since we had our first meeting with Mr. Arnold. He's long since retired, as have many of the teachers. Coach Chambers and Sandy Carter have passed away. A few of them are still there. But whatever their status, many of them continue to be our dear friends, even today.

We love those people, and we treasure those memories. Both were an indispensable part of our journey.

* For those who may not know or remember, former IU basketball coach Bob Knight was known for his volatile outbursts and actions. During one game vs. Purdue in 1985, in his frustration with the officiating, Knight grabbed a chair from the sidelines and flung it across the court. This incident received widespread national attention and became a legend in Indiana college basketball.

CHAPTER 5
HAIL PURDUE!

To some, this might seem a little strange to have an entire chapter on attending college football and basketball games. But for our family, following the fortunes of the Purdue Boilermaker football and basketball teams, whether on TV, in the news, or seeing a game or two in person a year, was part of the fabric of life in the Boone family.

Some of our fondest memories of our lives are of games seen in Ross Ade Stadium or Mackey Arena, and the fun we had—talking about the game, teasing, arguing, laughing, tailgating, throwing the football, rehashing, and more—on the way there and back. It became a tradition, a big part of our life as a family growing up and continuing today.

Of the scores of games we've attended over the years, the following are just a very few of the games and related experiences that made excursions to Purdue overflow with special memories and meaning for Peter and the rest of us.

Peter's First Game

It was the 1980–81 basketball season, and Purdue men's basketball was under the direction of new coach Gene Keady. A former Pittsburgh Steeler, Keady had brought a new emphasis on defense and an overall attitude of playing tough, hard-nosed, blue-collar basketball. While not overly talented, his first Boilermaker squad had overachieved, and they were fun to watch. I decided it was time for Roger and Peter to see a game at Mackey Arena.

In those early days, Peter was just five, and we didn't even worry about handicapped-accessible seating. He was still small enough that I just carried him up to wherever we were sitting and held him on my lap.

The first basketball game for the boys at Mackey was during the latter part of the season, and the opponent was Michigan State, under coach Jud Heathcoate. Games at Mackey are always fun, and this one was no exception. In the end, Purdue was able to pull out a hard-fought squeaker, winning by just a few points. After that first game, the boys were even more confirmed Boilermakers.

Peter may have only been five, but he had followed the Boilermakers all season and knew quite a bit about them. He knew that one of Purdue's star players was a prize freshman recruit named Russell Cross.

After the game, the Purdue players surprisingly just kind of lingered on the court, and jubilant fans eagerly made their way down to mingle and give congratulations. Roger and Peter wanted to know if we could go down, and they didn't have to twist my arm. As soon as we headed that way, Peter kept eagerly repeating and begging, over and over, "Dad, can we meet Russell Cross?"

I just told him "We'll have to see." Although clearly a budding star, the six feet eight African American Cross was one of those players who seemed to always have his "game face" on, and I wasn't at all sure how open he'd be to meeting little kids, but I thought we'd at least give it a try.

As we made our way over to him, we got lucky! He was just finishing talking with someone, and we obviously were going to get our chance. I stepped up to Russell and introduced myself, shaking hands with my free hand. Then I said, "I've got someone here who wants to meet you."

My fears quickly evaporated. Cross couldn't have been more congenial. I said, "This is Peter, and he is really looking forward to meeting you."

Cross smiled and said, "Hi, Peter, nice to meet you."

I held Peter up to say something in return, and he said nothing. Absolutely nothing! He just rested there on my arm with his mouth hanging open, saying nothing. I was embarrassed.

I tried again. "Peter, can you say 'hi' to Russell?" who was still being extremely nice.

Again, nothing. It quickly became obvious to me that Peter was intimidated. It wasn't like he'd never seen black kids. He'd known and interacted with many of them at White's. But he'd never seen one that was this big—a giant to him—and he didn't know how to handle it.

I finally just said something like, "I guess the cat must have his tongue tonight or something," thanked Russell for meeting with us— he still was being most gracious—and quickly took off.

So much for meeting Russell Cross.

Aerial Extravaganza and More

Purdue is known as the "Cradle of Quarterbacks," and during and after my college days, I've seen my share of good ones—Bob Griese, Mike Phipps, Gary Danielson, Mark Herrmann, Jim Everett, and Drew Brees for Purdue—and I'd also seen Jim Plunkett, Heisman Trophy winner for Stanford, and Joe Montana for Notre Dame.

I'd taken Roger to the Purdue-Notre Dame game in '79, but early fall of '81 was to be Peter's first game. We picked the Stanford game to go to, thought it sounded like it could be interesting, and I'd heard somewhere that they had a pretty good quarterback. Purdue had a pretty fair one that year in Scott Campbell. The game was nationally televised on ABC with Keith Jackson and Bob Griese calling the game.

Turned out Stanford's "pretty good quarterback" was the great John Elway! I'd really not heard much about him before that game, but of all the great quarterbacking I'd ever seen at Ross Ade, he put on the best performance ever! Campbell had a great game too. It was back and forth through the air and on the scoreboard the entire game. Purdue finally won an absolute thriller in the final moments.

All of us, boys included, had a blast. Games don't get any better than that.

A couple of other interesting sidelights—at that time, Purdue had a tradition that students would bring rolls of toilet paper to the game to use as streamers. After the first touchdown, the student section at the north end of the stadium would absolutely explode with thousands of rolls of toilet paper launched high into the air and land, partially unrolled in the north end zone.

Wanting the boys to have the experience of this unique ritual, we took our own four-pack of TP to the game. When it was Peter's turn to throw one, he threw it into the air as hard as he could, but it didn't go very high at all. As we watched its meager trajectory, it fell unceremoniously, largely unrolled, and hit a Coke vendor squarely in the head.

Another interesting minor facet of the game that the boys still talk about—Stanford is notorious for having a "nonconformist band." They were part of the halftime show, and as we watched them with the binoculars, and among other interesting and amazing phenomena, we discovered that one of the members was barefooted, band uniform jacket unbuttoned with no shirt, wearing a sombrero, and "playing" a vacuum cleaner, which was strung over his neck with a piece of clothesline cord. Weird, but added to our fun.

Hail Mary and Gopher Abuse

In 1998, Purdue football had a good coach, Joe Tiller, and a fast-rising young quarterback, Drew Brees, who were putting the program back on the national map. That year we decided to attend the Minnesota game in early October as a family.

By 1998, some things had changed in our world too. As the result of an emergency surgery to have part of a gangrenous bowel removed in 1990, Peter now had a colostomy bag.

On this particular day, Sandra couldn't go for some reason, so I drove, Peter was right behind me in his wheelchair, and Roger, now married to Tonya, and Phil were behind Pete. About the time we went through Delphi, Indiana, on the way to the game, I thought I could detect the faint but unmistakable odor of an ostomy leak.

At first I thought, *Surely not.* But as we went on, the smell grew stronger, and there was little doubt in my mind. When we got to Purdue, I drove down to the west end campus to a small shopping center. I told Roger, Tonya, and Phil to go on into Dairy Queen and get something to eat while I checked out Peter's situation.

Sure enough, my fears were reality. It wasn't a horrible mess yet, but the bag was coming loose, and, with ostomy bags, if you don't get the situation corrected sooner than later, you've got a rip-snorting disaster of epic proportions on your hands. The realization that Pete and I could quickly be in "deep do-do" was more than an idle figure of speech.

The only problem, Sandra and I pretty much tag-teamed on Peter's care, and she was the "ostomy specialist," and she wasn't there. I'd only changed it a few times, and under much better conditions than Peter sitting up in his wheelchair in the van. And that's before any of us had cell phones to call home for emergency instructions. I felt pretty much like a backup QB in fourth-and-twenty with the game on the line. We needed a "Hail Mary!" (desperation pass).

Frantically I dug into Pete's emergency supplies, got out the stuff I needed, and had Peter position himself as best he could while I contorted myself to try to take corrective action, standing bent over in the van. I worked feverishly for about twenty minutes, praying as hard as I could that he wouldn't have any further bowel movements until I could get the situation under control.

The Lord clearly heard my fervent pleas because much to my surprise, I was making significant headway. I got what mess there was cleaned up, got the new ostomy bag to actually adhere to his abdomen, and finished the job. I gave Pete a high-five and breathed a quick prayer of thanks!

I then charged into the DQ, washed my hands, grabbed a quick sandwich to go, got everyone loaded back up and headed for the stadium. We parked about a half mile away, walked as fast as we could, and got to the stadium just before kickoff.

Whatever challenges the first part of our day held, the rest of the day made up for it. Drew Brees went totally nuts, setting numerous

Big Ten passing records, as the Boilers blew out Minnesota 56–21. It was sheer fun!

And one more indelible memory of that game—for whatever reason, Minnesota's gopher mascot was being particularly obnoxious, majorly getting on the Purdue fans' nerves in the south end zone where we sat that day. The Boiler faithful responded back, pelting the gopher with wadded-up paper cups, and whatever they could throw at him.

But to this day, our kids still talk about how the Purdue cheerleaders finally got the gopher under control—they captured him right in front of us, each grasping an arm and leg, and rammed his groin against the goalpost.

That game had it all!

A True Friend

One year for Christmas, we got Peter Purdue season football tickets—one for him, and one for a driver/escort. Sandra and I also got a couple, but we'd typically go to a couple of games a year and sell the rest of ours. Peter, though, loved going and tried to go to every game he could. He loved the tickets, and it became an annual gift.

To get to the other games, he assembled a roster of Purdue fans and others who wanted to see a game a year and were willing to drive him and assist him as needed.

One of those was Dan Guenin, who had been one of Peter's sixth-grade teachers. Dan was a popular teacher, very sports-minded, and he and Pete had hit it off in elementary school, and had remained good friends ever since. Peter could usually count on Dan for a game a year, and when they went, they always had a good time.

One year after they got to the game, we got a call from Dan's cell phone. As they made their way across campus, they hit a bump, and Peter's wheelchair lost power. He was calling us for trouble-shooting assistance. We quickly ran through the list of possible solutions but found none that would work.

The only thing we could think of was to put Peter's chair in "free wheel," and it could then be pushed. But even then, a power chair with Peter in it weighed in the vicinity of four hundred pounds! We weren't about to ask Dan to do that, and told him he might as well just bring Pete home. But Dan wanted Peter to be able to see the game, and decided to just push him to the stadium anyway. However, after pushing him across the street and a couple hundred yards, the final approach to the southeast gate of Ross-Ade Stadium has about a fifty-yard incline. Somewhere during those fifty yards, the impact of Dan's decision hit home.

"I was in decent shape at the time, but it was a hot day, and about halfway up the incline, I was sweating profusely, and the muscles in my legs were quivering," he recalled. "I finally asked a couple other fans to help me, or we'd never have made it up to the stadium. It was quite an experience."

And Purdue wasn't the only place Dan took him. They went to away high school volleyball games and other events, and always had a great time together. One time they went to a Fellowship of Christian Athletes banquet in Fort Wayne to hear former Indianapolis Colts' coach Tony Dungy speak. Peter always had a knack for being able to finagle his way into meeting celebrities, and this occasion was no different. Coach Dungy was very gracious, and after they got to meet him and got a photo, Dan noticed him eyeing Peter as he moved away from the table.

"He's the toughest guy I've ever met," said Dan.

"I'll bet he is," said Coach Dungy.

No Good Deed Goes Unpunished

Ken Perkins, a friendly and outgoing guy, is a successful businessman in our church, and an Indiana University grad. Soon after Ken and his family started attending our church, he quickly noticed that Peter was a Purdue fan and began picking on him. Peter gave it right back, and they became good friends.

For many years, Ken was a sales manager for a major feed company, specializing in pig feed. One of his sales team, a former Purdue basketball player named Jon Kitchell, had a younger brother, Kelly, who was an offensive lineman for Purdue.

One time during the summer of 1999, Ken talked Kelly and a couple of his teammates, Sean Rufalo and Brady Doe, into coming to our house to meet Peter. He set this up with us, and it was a surprise to Pete.

After recovering from his initial amazement, Peter was jubilant! For an hour or more, Peter peppered them with questions, all about the inner workings of Purdue football. I even threw in a few questions of my own. The young men were all extremely gracious, and it was a great time.

To show his appreciation, Peter asked if Ken would like to accompany him to a Purdue football game to see Kelly play. Ken was an IU grad and really not that much of a sports fan, but said, "Sure, he'd be glad to go with Peter to a Purdue game." They went and had a good time.

The only thing, at the time of the visit Kelly was just coming off his redshirt freshman year and had four years of eligibility left. So Peter asked Ken to take him to a game all four of those seasons!

We told Ken he didn't have to, but even though he appeared to be getting more than he bargained for, he was a good sport about it. He took Peter to a game a year for the rest of Kelly's eligibility.

"For Peter, I was glad to do it," said Ken. "It actually wound up being fun. Those three guys were great about following up with Peter, so they'd tell him where to go after the game to meet players as they were coming out of the dressing room. So Peter got to know a lot of the players; he had cheerleaders coming up and hugging on him, and it was so cool. Those were good times."

A few years after that, Ken switched from feed sales to agricultural banking, and quickly became successful in that field, and a recognized leader in Indiana's ag community. Along the way, he also got involved in short-term missions work, and now regularly makes trips to a poor Asian country, to help people there learn pork production plus have an opportunity to share his Christian faith.

While on an Indiana agricultural trade mission to the Far East,

Ken met Jay Akridge, Purdue's dean of agriculture, and started working with Purdue to incorporate student interns into that ministry. Now sometimes Ken even wears Purdue shirts to church!

Peter would be overjoyed! No doubt he would also say this proves that God can help even IU people get on the right path.

Encouragement in the Bathroom

One time several years ago, we were at Mackey Arena for a men's basketball game. Tipoff was coming up soon, and there was the usual hustle, bustle, and excitement in the concourse as people hurried to their seats, with the sounds of the pep band inside the arena filling the entire building, getting the fans fired up.

Peter had just finished using the restroom, which was packed. He went to wash his hands, but the sink was one of those that was sort of accessible, but not all that much. He couldn't reach to the back of it to turn on the faucet. So I was helping him wash his hands.

While I was doing that, I felt a hand grasp my shoulder firmly, then release it. I was just about done helping Pete, so in a couple of seconds I turned around, expecting to see some Purdue fan from our church, or Wabash, or someone else I knew.

But no one was there—absolutely no one.

It was really mysterious. If it was someone we knew, surely they would have stayed there until we got done. But why would someone do that, then just suddenly disappear, which whoever it was had obviously done?

Peter and I then headed to our seats, but still it perplexed me. Finally I concluded that the only possibility must have been that it was some stranger who had seen me helping Peter, and had put his hand on my shoulder as an affirming gesture, and then made a hasty retreat, not wanting any recognition.

If that was the case—and I could think of no other—it certainly accomplished its goal. It really did feel very good; it was very affirming, really made me feel appreciated. And what I was doing was, very literally, no big deal at all. I was just helping Peter wash his hands.

My best guess is that it was someone who had a background with disabilities, saw the two of us, and just wanted to give me an anonymous "good job, buddy," then leave before we could see who he was.

One of my favorite Mark Twain quotes is, "I could live for two months on a good compliment." Whoever you are out there, it's been several years now, and your thoughtful gesture still warms my heart whenever I think of it.

CHAPTER 6
1982: FOUR KEY EVENTS

As Peter was growing up, we had years that were much more eventful than 1982. But a number of events that year marked turning points in our journey with Peter and as a family.

Cross that One off the List

The first was that I finally finished my master's degree in counseling from Ball State University. I'd begun it in 1978, taking about a class per quarter. But at some point, I began to feel like that was going to take forever. So my last year I doubled up on classes for something of a sprint to the finish. Peter was in the hospital for a couple of weeks in the early spring, and I took a few days off and did some of my studying while I stayed with him. In May 1982, I was exhausted, but I was done!

I'd originally begun the program to get more credentialing for my work at White's, to get a diploma to hang on the wall. But I was pleasantly surprised in that I genuinely learned a lot more than I ever imagined. The things I learned were extremely helpful to me in working with kids, staff, and others in my work at White's. But I also benefitted a lot personally.

You can't go through a counseling program without learning a lot about yourself—what makes you tick, why you got to be the way you are, how you can probably change some things but not others, the importance of articulating your feelings with someone else, when to seek help, some strategies for dealing with the stresses in your life, and much more.

Sometime about 1980, I'd made the decision that I either needed to drop the program or hit it hard and get it done. I worked my tail off to do the latter, and have never had any regrets. Even in my post-White's days, I still use the things I learned back then on a daily basis. And through the years that followed, with the emotional roller coaster ride that came with being Peter's parent, having that background was a blessing

Discovering a Mentor

The summer after I finished my counseling program, I finally had some free time, and I decided to do a little catching up on my spiritual life and growth. During that summer, I read *Mere Christianity* by C. S. Lewis, and for me it was a "wow" experience. In Lewis, I found a new mentor—someone who, like me, had a skeptical nature and had nevertheless found that Christianity really did make sense. He could take Christianity and explain it in a logical way that really resonated with me, that made it even more real, more relevant, and more meaningful.

I was also struck by the obvious joy with which Lewis lived his life, and the way he lived it for others. In numerous ways he challenged me, roughly twenty years after his death, to be a better person, a better Christian.

After reading *Mere Christianity,* I soon devoured *The Screwtape Letters, Letters to an American Lady,* and more. Lewis was to become a lifelong influence on me.

Of the many things he said that impacted me, one originated out of his service in the British Army in World War I. Lewis had allowed himself to be drafted for that conflict, and it made an indelible impression on him.

Although I've searched high and low for that quote, I haven't been able to find it in Lewis's extremely prolific writings. But I remember the gist of it with extreme clarity. He said that he had always had an appreciation for the "good draftees," those soldiers who were drafted, rather than volunteered. Even though it was not their choice, once they had been called, they had nevertheless taken their mission to heart and served well and nobly.

That thought really helped me. As much as Sandra and I loved Peter, there were times when we nevertheless chafed under the burden of his never-ending care, hospitalizations, doctor appointments, and the myriad disruptions to our lives. I could relate to Lewis's comments. I didn't sign up for this.

But to reframe that into seeing Peter's care not just as a burden, but a chance to "serve nobly" brought a new perspective that I seriously needed. Seeing that care as an honor to which we had been called made it easier to "keep on keeping on" in the many years that followed.

A Home Away from Home

One event that was a real lifesaver for us was the opening of the Indiana Ronald McDonald House in Indianapolis in October 1982. Prior to that, when Sandra and I would be staying with Peter at the hospital, where we slept was a considerable problem. We didn't have enough money to stay in a nearby hotel on a regular basis.

So sometimes one of us could stay with Peter in his room. Sometimes we slept on a couch or in a chair in the surgery waiting lounge, sometimes on a bench nearby a waiting area, and sometimes on the floor of the hospital chapel. (But I've been kicked out of there more than once when discovered by night security). There were times I slept on the floor of our van in the parking lot during warmer weather. But then someone told me that in that part of town, I was lucky I hadn't had my throat slit. When we couldn't stand it anymore, we'd finally spring for a night in the cheapest motel we could find in the area.

When the Ronald McDonald house opened, it was a godsend! It was a beautiful facility, not far from Riley or Methodist Hospitals. The rooms were beautiful. We had our own section of a refrigerator where we could buy some groceries, do our own cooking, and really have something of a little "home away from home." And all for only ten bucks a night!

They even had activities and things to do and play with for siblings of the hospitalized child. Philip loved staying at the Ronald McDonald House.

Sometimes church groups would come in and put on a meal for a special occasion. Not only was the food great, it was provided with a loving touch from people who cared, to people who needed some caring.

Even the architecture promoted rest and healing. Its beauty inspired. Its functionality nudged families to get to know each other and share each other's burden, yet didn't force it if they weren't up to it.

And over the years, we learned that when a loved one is in the hospital, it really is important for the caregivers to take care of themselves. With all that's going on in your life, it's amazing what a shower, change of clothes, a good night's sleep, good meals, a little exercise, and something of a regular routine can do for your mental health. And make you more effective in being there for your loved one.

Sometimes today I get really upset with the food activists who target McDonald's, particularly their efforts to demonize and beat up on Ronald McDonald, as some villainous, pied piper leading a generation of children into a life of obesity.

McDonald's is an American business that has been successful in providing products and services people obviously find enjoyable. Yes, childhood obesity is a problem, but I don't see where beating up on Ronald is the answer. I think parents taking responsibility to teach their children how to make good choices, get some exercise, and balance Big Macs with moderation is effort better spent.

When McDonald's decided to sponsor Ronald McDonald Houses, they did a wonderful thing. They've been a good corporate citizen. They've helped countless thousands of families who were in a very tough spot. We were one of them, and we'll be eternally grateful. God bless you, Ronald.

Turning "Scars into Stars"

We discovered something else at the Ronald McDonald House. When we were staying there on a weekend, we weren't able to attend church services, and really felt the need for some spiritual nourishment, even if it did come from a TV. It was during one of these times that we discovered Robert Schuller, and the *Hour of Power*, from the Crystal Cathedral in California.

Schuller was an excellent preacher who took a very positive approach toward Christianity and said his was a "counseling ministry." There were times when I felt he mixed in too much psychology with his theology. But over a number of years, either at the Ronald McDonald House, or at home, on those occasions where we were too exhausted or too numb to attend services at our own church, Schuller preached countless sermons that spoke directly to our need, hitting the exact spot where we were hurting. One of Schuller's practices was to take pithy nuggets of encouragement and package them in simple, catchy wording that was easy to remember. Things such as: "Let your hopes, not your hurts, shape your future;" "Tough times never last, but tough people do;" "Turn your scars into stars;" "God's delays are not God's denials;" "Press on. Obstacles are seldom the same size tomorrow as they are today;" and "What appears to be the end of the road may simply be a bend in the road."

For years, his messages and many encouraging admonitions comforted, inspired, nurtured, and blessed us during some of our darkest hours.

CHAPTER 7
1984: IT IS WELL

In 1949, British author George Orwell had written a classic novel, *1984*. In his book, Orwell had predicted a world full of dire developments, including perpetual war, "Big Brother," and widespread persecution. As the year 1984 approached, pundits speculated on what, if any, ominous developments would in fact happen, now that that long-speculated-on year was nearly upon us.

For our family, that year really did turn out to be a year to remember, for both some good and not-so-good reasons.

***

The year started out well enough. The boys were now thirteen, nine, and five, and for a variety of reasons, we'd never taken all of them on a "road vacation." So as soon as school was out, we headed for a ten-day traveling vacation, beginning at Wisconsin Dells. We spent a few days there, splitting our time between the scenic wonders and the other kid-friendly attractions of the area.

Then we headed for Green Bay, home of my favorite pro football team. Unbeknown to us, we arrived right in the middle of their spring minicamp. It was a great opportunity to see a real NFL team practice, plus we had opportunities to see the players up close, get pictures, autographs, and talk with them.

The boys loved visiting the Packer Hall of Fame, and Roger, Philip, and I sneaked onto Lambeau Field with a football to "score a few touchdowns and extra points," for which we were soon summarily kicked out. (Peter couldn't get onto the field on this occasion, but got a real hoot out of seeing the rest of us get booted).

Next we headed up through the Upper Peninsula of Michigan, made a brief excursion into Canada, then camped out in a tent for a couple of nights at the Straits State Park, right next to the Mackinac Bridge. During the day, we took the ferry over to Mackinac Island.

All of us had a lot of fun. It was a great trip.

Trouble Brewing

Not long after we got home, Peter began having some headaches. We made an appointment with his new pediatric neurosurgeon, Dr. Michael Turner, who had taken over some of Dr. Feuer's caseload. After running some tests, Dr. Turner told us that Peter had a condition known as the Chiari malformation, in which Peter's brain stem had settled lower into his spinal cord area. Not one to rush into things, Dr. Turner said we needed to keep a close eye on things, but told us that it might require surgery at some point.

In July we went on our annual extended family vacation to Lake Wawasee with Sandra's family. Peter's headaches had gradually gotten worse, but while we were on vacation, the pace really picked up. Rather than hanging out at the beach with his cousins, Peter felt bad enough that he just stayed in our cottage most of the time, and he and I played a lot of chess.

During some of the games, a headache would come over him in the upper part of his neck, and he'd start crying out in agony, and Peter was no crybaby. It was heartbreaking. Then, almost as quickly as it had come on, the headache would subside. He began having multiple episodes of this daily.

We hadn't planned to see Dr. Turner again until after we were home from the lake, but felt we had no choice but to call him. He sounded very concerned and made an appointment for Peter to see Dr. David McClone of Chicago's Children's Hospital to get a second opinion. Sandra and I loaded Peter up and headed for Chicago, leaving Roger and Philip with her parents.

We knew of Dr. McClone from reading the spina bifida newsletters, and knew that he was one of the foremost neurosurgeons in the world for spina bifida. When we met him, he was small in stature, and appeared to be in his fifties. For all his notable accomplishments, we found him to be a very humble and caring person.

Dr. McClone ran some more scans, studied them carefully, and observed Peter closely. He then said that Dr. Turner was correct in his diagnosis and anticipation of Peter needing surgery.

"I'm particularly concerned about Peter's respiration," he said. "The pressure on Peter's brainstem is interfering with his ability to breathe."

He briefly described the surgery that Peter would need as a "spinal decompression," in which some small pieces of bone would need to be removed from his top vertebrae and skull, in order to relieve the pressure.

He didn't say it, but he didn't have to—this was big-league stuff, the biggest challenge yet of Peter's young life. He said he'd call Dr. Turner to schedule it for the next morning, and that we needed to get to Indianapolis as soon as we could. We left immediately, sped down I-65, and arrived at Indianapolis Methodist Hospital late that evening.

Surgery and Aftermath

Peter had his surgery early the next morning. It lasted several hours, but when Dr. Turner finally came out, he felt optimistic about how things had gone. He cautioned us that the next few days were crucial. He said Peter would be in ICU for three or four days, and then return to a regular room for a few more days.

Initially, things went well, and we were encouraged. So far, the surgery seemed to have eliminated his headaches, and he was moved to a regular room. By this time, I'd returned home and back to work, and Sandra was staying with him.

Then one day I got a call at work from Sandra. Something was drastically wrong. He'd woken up feeling awful, and his temperature had spiked to 105 degrees. They'd done lab work to see what was going on.

When the results came back, there was nothing that could have prepared us for the results. However it had happened, Peter had meningitis. To be recovering from a delicate brain surgery, only to come up with a potentially lethal infection that could doom everything was big-time trouble.

Peter was immediately put on heavy-duty, high-dose, IV antibiotics, which he'd be on for a couple of weeks. At the end of that time, the IVs were removed. But again, Peter spiked a high temperature and became very sick, and the IVs had to be resumed.

This was to become a pattern that was to be repeated over and over. Ultimately, he spent the better part of three months in the hospital fighting this battle. Sandra stayed with him almost all of that time, while I tried to work at home, and keep our other balls in the air.

As he went through this ordeal, Peter would really feel pretty decent while he was on the IVs. In characteristic fashion, he kept in good spirits, and even helped the rest of us do the same, in his own unique, Peter sort of way. One day when I was staying with him I'd bought him an *Indianapolis Star,* and he was lying in bed reading the sports page.

"Hey Dad, listen to this," he said. "There's an article in here about some woman who shot her husband because she said he was watching too much football. It's a good thing Mom's not like that, huh?"

He kept up with his school work. He and Sandra received a steady stream of visits from family, Southwood teachers, friends, our pastor Dave Phillips, church family and others, as well as a ton of cards and notes of encouragement. One member of our church, Dan Vanderpool, was the Wabash Circuit Court judge at the time, and even sent Peter an official court order, ordering him to get well and get home as soon as possible!

Earlier that year, the Baltimore Colts had made their infamous midnight getaway to become the Indianapolis Colts. Peter was visited by various Colts during his stay, and hit it off pretty well with future Pro Bowl tackle Chris Hinton, who said he'd get him tickets for a game as soon as he was able.

Through the course of the lengthening hospital stay, Peter never complained. At all. On days when he was feeling good, he'd go to the playroom and make crafts with the playroom lady. Or watch sports. Or banter with his nurses about Purdue and IU. Sometimes when he was resting, he'd just pat Sandra on the arm, and say, "I love you, Mom."

Over time, the hospital stay really began to wear on her. I'd get down as often as I could, and take Roger and Philip when I could. On our wedding anniversary, I took the boys, plus "Joe," a White's student who had earned an off-campus excursion. I left them with Peter while I took Sandra on a carriage ride in downtown Indy. Then on the way home, we stopped at a White Castle, and I told the boys they could get as many of the infamous mini-sandwiches as they could eat. Philip ate six, I ate ten, Roger ate fifteen, and Joe ate twenty.

We were trying to make the best of our situation and have a little fun as we could. But overall, it wasn't looking good.

It Is Well

On one of those week nights I hurried down to Indianapolis for the evening, just to spend a couple of hours with Peter and Sandra. I was driving home, and I was extremely discouraged. While at the hospital, I had tried to be upbeat for Sandra and Peter. I thought I'd been reasonably successful in pulling off that act while I was there. But now I was on my way home, and there was no fooling myself.

We were in a mess. He'd do okay while on the antibiotics, but every time the doctors tried to remove them, he regressed quickly. He couldn't live on antibiotics as a long-term strategy, but it didn't appear he could live off of them.

It was one of the most horrible, rotten, helpless feelings I'd ever experienced. My child was in a terrible situation, and there was absolutely nothing we could do about it. I saw absolutely no good end in sight.

I tried to pray a number of times, but felt like my words were just bouncing off the inside of the van windshield. I didn't feel like listening to the radio, didn't feel like doing much of anything, just kept driving toward home. I wished I could just cry, but no tears would come. I was just too numb, too tired, too whatever.

When I got home, Roger and Philip were staying with the Rich and Sandy Davis' family for the night, and I was there by myself. It was late, and I was tired but didn't feel like going to bed yet either. For whatever reason, I put on an album of hymns and started listening.

Three or four songs into the album, the familiar strains of "It Is Well with My Soul" started playing. That was one of my favorite hymns, but on that night, it spoke to me in a way it never had before.

The second verse goes:

"Tho' Satan should buffet, tho' trials should come, let this blest assurance control,

That Christ hath regarded my helpless estate, and shed his own blood for my soul."

"Helpless!" That word nailed it, describing exactly what I was feeling that night. I don't know that I'd ever felt more helpless than I had on this occasion. But suddenly it was okay. Because as the song assured me, Jesus himself had "been there, done that," and cared enough about me that he'd not only shed his blood for me, I had a mental picture of him also shedding tears for me, right at that moment.

When my tears came, they didn't stop for a long time. It was the most profusely I'd wept in years. I couldn't believe the relief it brought. I played the hymn again, and wept some more.

Then finally the tears stopped. Like a summer rain on a hot and sticky evening, they'd cleared the air, freshened things.

I had no assurance that Peter was going to miraculously get well or turn around from his desperate situation. God didn't speak to me, audibly or otherwise. But I felt an incredible, unexplainable peace that I hadn't felt in months.

"Whatever my lot, thou hast taught me to say, it is well, it is well, with my soul."

(Lyrics by Horatio G. Spafford)

Returning Home

After about three months in the hospital, the infection doctors again took Peter off the antibiotics. As we waited and prayed for a better result, but without much real hope, after about three days nothing dire had occurred yet; they told us they were going to try sending him home and see what happened.

As we arrived home, one of our neighbors, Colleen Spencer, had put a banner up on a couple of stakes in our yard, saying "Welcome Home Peter." As appreciative as I was of her efforts, I had little hope that we were going to be there long.

As the days passed, I kept waiting for the "other shoe to drop" and for Peter to spike another temperature, get seriously ill, and have to make a fast trip back to Methodist Hospital. But one day passed, then another, then another. It didn't happen. He regained his strength, returned to school, and, for Peter, pretty much returned to "normal." Free of headaches, and free of meningitis.

To this day, we don't know why he recovered on that occasion after so many failures on previous tries. I'm sure the thousands of prayers that went up for him played a part. But God really does work in mysterious ways, and whatever the reason, it was great to have Peter and Sandra home again. We had much to be thankful for.

Putting Things in Perspective

One day later that year, I was at a ball game at Southwood, and one of White's staff members, Mel Weaver, came up and started talking to me.

"You know, sometimes I think I've got problems," he said. "But then I look at Peter and all he's been through, and how he has such a great attitude and is always smiling and happy. It makes me think, if Peter can do that, then why can't I?"

It was a comment Sandra and I were to hear countless times over the years. Peter had that effect on people.

"Decomposed Neck"

Sandra's always had a funny way of mixing her words and metaphors. When we first got married, I was amazed to learn that freestone peaches became "Firestone" peaches, and "writing on the wall," or "reading between the lines," got spliced into "reading between the walls," and more. The boys and I have always had fun teasing her no end about these gaffes, saying that for her, English is a second language. To which she responds, "Whatever. You know what I mean."

Some time after Peter's surgery, she made some comment about him having had a "spinal decomposition."

Spinal decomposition?

"Do you realize that you just said that Peter has a 'rotten, decaying neck'?" I asked. "He had a spinal *decompression*."

"Whatever. You know what I mean."

From then on, when she'd get on Peter's case about something he should have done, or done better, we'd always remind her, "Just a minute. What do you expect of a boy with a 'decomposed neck'?"

"Whatever. You know what I mean."

Peter loved it! During those times, it was kind of fun to have a "decomposed neck."

CHAPTER 8
1987: GAME CHANGER

It was 1987, and Peter was in his twelfth year. After 1984, we'd had three relatively "normal" years—for Peter—with him doing well in school, now in fifth grade, and generally enjoying life. But Dr. Lindseth's prediction from a few years earlier—that when kids with spina bifida hit their growth spurt, all kinds of things can happen—began to kick in.

We'd begun to notice some symptoms that concerned us. His speech was a little harder to understand, and his handwriting had deteriorated noticeably. An MRI showed that he had another cyst on his spinal cord at the base of his brain. A couple of times earlier, Dr. Turner had done surgeries to correct similar cysts, where a tube is inserted into the cyst to drain excess spinal fluid and relieve pressure, and, in each case, that had done the job.

Now it was time to do it again. We scheduled the surgery at Indianapolis Methodist Hospital for spring break, so as to not miss any more school than he had to. The surgery was scheduled for April 9, which happened to be Roger's birthday.

***

After the surgery, our neurosurgeon, Dr. Turner, said everything had gone well. But when Peter came out of recovery, he couldn't talk. Initially Sandra and I didn't think too much about it, just figured it was probably some kind of reaction to the anesthesia or something.

But soon some other symptoms showed themselves. He couldn't swallow, couldn't eat normally, and had to be fed through an NG tube. Again, all of us, including Dr. Turner, thought this was a temporary reaction to the surgery. We couldn't have been more wrong.

As the days wore on, the symptoms not only continued, but there were more of them. Peter had been on a ventilator immediately after surgery. But whenever they would try to remove the ventilator for any length of time, he'd get very drowsy and lethargic and have to go back on it. At some point, we learned that none of these symptoms were just temporary reactions.

The brain and spinal cord are very sensitive areas, and it became apparent that during the surgery there had been some kind of brain trauma that had also affected his breathing. He could breathe okay when he was awake, but whenever he'd go to sleep, even for a nap, his brain didn't make him breathe deeply enough to expel the carbon dioxide, which led to a dangerous buildup of that gas in his bloodstream.

The hospitalization went on for several weeks, as the doctors tried gamely to come up with answers that never materialized. For most of the time, Peter was pretty occupied with trying to just get better and regain his strength. He really didn't seem to focus too much on the implications of what appeared to be a whole new direction in his life.

But for Sandra and I, as it sunk in that those functions that all of us take for granted—talking, swallowing, eating, breathing on our own—not only hadn't come back, but appeared increasingly unlikely to ever come back, we were shocked and devastated.

As for me, I was entering a period which would reoccur numerous times over the next few years, which our pastor, Dave Phillips, referred to as the "dark night of the soul." I'm not sure of the exact definition of that phrase, but am pretty sure this was one of them.

As we'd gone through previous crises, I had usually considered myself to be pretty strong. But this time it was more than I could handle. How could something like this happen? How am I going to be able to stand not seeing our child, who had already overcome so much, and had developed such a marvelous, coping attitude—Chief Running Mouth—not be able to talk? How is Peter—Mr. Sociable—going to be able to interact with others in any kind of a meaningful way? How am I going to be able to stand seeing him not being able to enjoy cheeseburgers, french fries, and pizza anymore? How is he going to be able to do school, which he loves? How are we, and Peter, going to be able to handle this? Is he even going to survive this one? What if he doesn't? And then again, what if he does?

And what about Sandra and me, and even Roger and Philip? Hadn't we already endured enough? Wasn't it enough that we'd been "blessed" with a child with spina bifida? Is this some kind of a cruel joke? And what about God? Is he sleeping on the job? Doesn't he care that we're drowning in our own tears? Doesn't he care that this precious, lovable little eleven-year-old who's already overcome so much adversity is losing some of the few things that he enjoys most in life? Maybe God's getting too old for the job.

Those were just a few of the questions on my "list." The answers were not quickly forthcoming. Some of them took years to resolve.

***

After several weeks, we were finally released from the hospital. In most of Peter's previous hospital releases, we'd gone home with the problem reasonably "fixed" or at least on the way. But this was a whole new ballgame.

By this time, he'd had a couple of more surgeries to put in a feeding tube and tracheostomy. And he was going to have to be on a ventilator at night and oxygen the rest of the day. Since he couldn't swallow, he was going to have to have a suction machine to suction out the secretions from his mouth and throat. He got all of his nutrition, in liquid form, through his feeding tube, with the assistance of a feeding pump that ran all night long. I'd always thought of these types of measures as "life support" interventions, but our doctors assured us that Peter was not terminal, but could still live a productive life with the help of these devices.

When we got home, Peter (and Philip's) room essentially became a small intensive care unit, complete with big oxygen tanks, and beepers and alarms for every new device. And we were introduced to a home health supplier, who made biweekly deliveries of liquid feeding, oxygen, trach and feeding tube supplies, and more. We had to coordinate all of these measures. All this had taken Peter's care—already considerable—to a whole different level. Sandra was an excellent nurse, and also great at managing all of Peter's care, so together we just pitched in and did what we had to do. All of this was overwhelming at first, but we gradually learned our new tasks and routines, and our "new life" became more routine.

Eating: How Do We Do It?

On the first day we got home, when it was time for our first meal together, we weren't sure how to go about it. Sandra and I had eaten our meals in the hospital cafeteria while Peter was there, but now that we were home, we were both still heartsick over the fact that Peter could no longer eat normally. On one hand, we hated to eat in front of him when he couldn't be a participant. On the other hand, we had to eat ourselves, not much way around that. So what do we do? Eat in front of him, even when he couldn't? Or just have him go to his room so he didn't have to watch us? That didn't seem right. This was a real dilemma for us, and whatever we did, we didn't want to get it wrong, didn't want to hurt Peter. I don't think this one was in any of the parenting books.

Not knowing what to do, I finally just said to Peter, "Pete, it's time for supper, and we're not sure what to do here. The truth is that we have to eat. But we feel bad for you that you can't, and don't want you to feel bad having to watch us. What do you want to do?"

"That's okay. I really don't mind," he mouthed and gestured to us. "I just want to be out here with you guys."

And that was it. So simple, so matter of fact, so common sense, so Peter. So that's the way we did it.

Coming to Grips

Given our "new normal," we quickly had to figure out some new ways to communicate, and fast. We quickly became fairly adept at reading Peter's lips. Between doing that and his body language and facial expressions that accompanied it, that worked pretty well for the most part. And if there was something that we couldn't comprehend, Pete would either write it down on a note, or spell it out, kind of like on an imaginary blackboard in front of him. We'd been told that when Pete got better, and the dust settled, that were some adaptive language devices that might be of help. But for now, we were getting by.

Sandra and I were both concerned about how Peter was handling his new situation emotionally. For all his life, disability was normal enough for him that he took just about everything in stride, dealt with it, and tried to live as normally as possible. But this was new territory, and even for Peter, anything but normal.

I was trained as a counselor but felt wholly inadequate to deal with Pete on this. When I'd help him get ready for bed, he wasn't his usual talkative, laughing self. Instead he seemed far away, lost in his own thoughts. There were some occasions where I'd try to talk with him about it, and say something like, "Peter, there's a lot that's happened to you lately. Would you like to talk about it?" But he really didn't seem to want to. It appeared to me that he was just trying to process it all, and try to wrap his brain and emotions around it.

***

I'm very aware that in today's world, many people experiencing what we had would be thinking lawsuit. It never crossed our minds. We knew from years of previous experience that Dr. Turner was an excellent neurosurgeon, in Indianapolis's best neurosurgery practice. He himself initiated a second opinion in 1984, before Peter had undergone the spinal decompression, and the world-famous Dr. McClone had confirmed everything he'd recommended to us. Dr. Turner was also very good with Peter, cared deeply about him, and would never give Peter anything than his best effort. Peter liked him and so did we.

But just because someone is an excellent surgeon doesn't mean that every surgery goes right every time. The brainstem is a very delicate piece of the body, and we knew ahead of time that bad things were a possibility. We also knew that we had no real choice but to address Peter's increasingly serious spinal cord problems. To us, the delicate nature of the surgery on a sensitive part of the brain was the likely culprit. Life is a risk.

In my opinion, there's way too much suing going on today, a good part of it motivated by greed. There's a place for legal recourse in cases of gross negligence or incompetence. Sandra and I always took the approach that we expected Peter's doctors to be good, not perfect. Even for pitchers who throw perfect games, not every pitch is a strike.

Dr. Turner felt badly for us, and we felt badly for him. He continued to be an excellent physician for Peter, and did great work with him for decades to come.

And There Was More

As eventful as the first half of 1987 had been for us, there was more to come. Because of the serious defect in Peter's spine, as he began to get closer to his teen years, his spine started going off in all directions. Pete's orthopedic doctor, Dr. Lindseth, had been telling us for some time that Peter had both scoliosis—where the spine grows crooked sideways—but also kyphosis, where it grows forward in a curve.

He had told us that he would have to do a spinal fusion at some point to stabilize Peter's spine, or that the curvatures would eventually squash his internal organs, seriously jeopardize his quality of life, and even endanger his life. Unfortunately, the situation had progressed quickly enough that Peter needed to have the surgery as soon as possible, even though he was still in a considerably weakened condition from his surgeries earlier that year.

The surgery was scheduled for August 5 at Riley Children's Hospital in Indianapolis. It would involve reinforcing his spine with bone tissue from a "bone bank," then stabilizing the spine by attaching steel rods to his spine until the fusion had solidified. Dr. Lindseth advised us that was a big-time surgery, probably the biggest of Peter's young life, and involved no small amount of risk. On the other hand, Peter's spine was growing in multiple directions at a rate such that we had no choice.

The day of the surgery started early and was one of the longest days of our lives. The surgery started at about eight in the morning, and went on until about seven that evening—a new record, even for Peter. Sandra's parents and our pastor, Dave Phillips, were with us for the whole time.

I figured that when they got done, Dr. Lindseth and his team would be exhausted, but it was the opposite. After the initial briefing, in which Dr. Lindseth said things had gone well, we saw the team in the hall a little later, and they seemed very energized, like they'd just accomplished "the big one." We saw that as a good sign.

Even though the "big one" had gone well, Peter was still going to require several weeks of hospitalization, essentially on bed rest with minimal movement, to let the his spine do the actual work of fusing.

Alarming Situation

Peter's hospitalization just happened to coincide with the 1987 Pan Am Games, which were held in Indianapolis, which was a very big deal for the city. Many of the events were held on the IUPUI campus, just a few blocks from Riley Hospital.

One Sunday afternoon was a pretty, sunny, lazy day, and I was staying at the hospital with Peter by myself. He and I were just relaxing, watching a basketball game, when he got some visitors. It was one of his friends from our church youth group, Sherri Shugart, and her mother, Kathy. Even though Sherri was about three years older than Peter, they were very good friends. But although they were "just friends," Sherri was pretty cute, and Peter secretly had a crush on her.

Sherri and Kathy hadn't much more than said "hi" and sat down, when just about every alarm in Peter's ICU room monitors started going off big time. I thought to myself that this is strange; everything really seems okay. Seconds later, three or four nurses came running into the room to see what all the commotion was about.

As they checked it out, turns out the only problem in the room was Sherri. As soon as she got there, Peter's heart rate, blood pressure, respiration, and just about every other vital statistic that was capable of setting off an alarm had done just that. Everyone had a good laugh, and the nurses just put the alarms on silence for the duration of Sherri's visit. If Peter's crush on Sherri had been a secret before, it was no longer. The alarms had blown his cover!

***

As 1987 wound down, Peter eventually got out of the hospital. In October, he was finally able to return to regular school. For all our fears about how he would cope, his wheelchair loaded up with oxygen tanks and other new devices, and not being able to talk, he seemed to at least be doing okay, communicating and otherwise.

Sandra and I continued to struggle with our "new normal," and with the losses that had taken place in Peter's life the past few months. I think in some respects it was harder for us as parents to see our child lose some of his key abilities than it was for Peter. I often wished that I could just take all of Peter's problems and trade places with him. Also, I had known for many years that when it gets down to it, we don't have nearly as much control over things in our lives as we like to think. But 1987 had sledgehammered that point home with unmistakable certainty.

Although I should have learned by now that God had been faithful to us, I was a slow learner, and our new normal had reopened old wounds. I continued to seek answers to why awful things like this happen to great kids like Peter. I read C. S. Lewis's *The Problem of Pain,* and Philip Yancey's *Where Is God When It Hurts?* Each helped some, but not completely by any means. I reread the book of Job in the Bible. I hadn't read it for a while, and found it very interesting that for all of Job's troubles and questions, he never did get any of them answered. God wasn't inclined to answer the question of suffering for Job, and apparently he hadn't changed his approach any in the millenniums since. I found myself in the paradoxical position of being both frustrated with God and yet more dependent on him than ever.

One thing that weighed on us mightily was the fact that we really thought we were losing Peter. By the end of the year, he still really didn't look that good, and with all his newfound challenges, neither Sandra nor I could imagine how he could possibly live much longer. We were in something of a grief mode, essentially preparing to lose our child. I also had to balance all of this with the demands of a stressful job.

Given that we didn't think we had much time left with him, I wanted to be able to take Pete to at least one more Purdue basketball game at Mackey Arena. I tried to get some tickets for the Christmas break, preconference game with Kansas State, but none were to be had. I wrote my best tear-jerker letter to the Purdue ticket office explaining our situation, and they really came through for us. Peter and I got front row seats—the best we'd ever had—and he enjoyed the game thoroughly, just like old times. Before the game, Assistant Athletic Director Bob King came over and wished Peter well.

But the thing that helped me more than anything was Peter himself. For all of the year's difficulties, he never once complained, never asked why, never showed any signs of self-pity, never lost his ability to enjoy what of life he could, and never appeared to worry unduly about those things he couldn't control. After he'd ruminated on his new situation for a while, he'd apparently come to terms with it, and had decided to go ahead and enjoy and make the best of what he had left.

One night when I was helping him get ready for bed, it hit me. *If Peter's handling this situation—and he's the main one with the problems—then what's my problem?* Seeing the situation from that perspective made an abrupt change in my thinking and attitude, and helped me turn the corner during that chapter of my life.

I've mentioned before that for all his limitations, Peter had the heart and soul of an athlete. The greatest athletes—the Peyton Mannings, the Larry Birds, the LeBron James—are the ones who have the gift of making those lesser players around them rise to the challenge, and play better than they ever thought they could. Peter did that with me.

CHAPTER 9
SNAPSHOTS OF A "NUTHOUSE"

Compared to a lot of families, our household was fairly chaotic. I was a supervisor in a large residential treatment center for troubled kids, and my job was demanding, including long hours, lots of on-call time, and crisis intervention. Sandra worked part time as one of the White's nurses. We had Peter, who had a never-ending string of medical challenges and hospitalizations. And we also had Roger and Philip, who were four years older and younger than Peter, respectively, and had their own lives and activities. Roger once described our home, not totally inaccurately, as a "nuthouse."

But Sandra and I nevertheless tried to make our home life as "normal" as we could under the circumstances. And have some fun along the way. Here are just a few peeks into our home during those days.

Brotherly Love

In books on birth order phenomena, the oldest child is typically reliable and conscientious, which would reasonably describe Roger. Last borns are typically social beings, the clowns, which would pretty well describe Philip. Middle borns, by comparison, are the ones who typically are the "neglected ones," who tend to get somewhat overlooked by the attention given the first and last children.

In our case, Peter, with the care he required, obliterated that stereotype. As they were growing up, both Roger and Philip had times where they felt Peter encroached on what should have been their allotment of parental or others' attention, and probably with some justification. Living with a brother like Peter was not unlike living with a proverbial elephant in the house.

But for the most part, Roger and Philip handled their situations pretty well. And for the most part, they got along pretty much like most brothers—okay most of the time, somewhat less than that at other times. After the "statute of limitations of adulthood" had kicked in, I learned about some things that had happened during those years.

***

Peter was always a good kid, but by no means an angel. Roger told me that there was one time when they were kids, and he'd gotten frustrated with Peter and punched him in the shoulder. It made Peter mad, so when Roger was in the shower, Peter went into his room, tore up his Larry Bird basketball cards and threw them on the floor.

"I wanted to tell you and Mom so bad, but I couldn't," said Roger. "I figured if you found out that I'd punched Peter in a wheelchair, you'd kill me, so I couldn't say anything about it. Peter wound up getting the last word on that one."

On another occasion—all these things happened while Sandra and I were out of the house—Peter was doing something to annoy both Roger and Philip, so they figured out a way to encourage more cooperative behavior on his part.

"We stuck a broomstick through the lower spokes in his wheelchair, grounding him until he agreed to quit bugging us," said Roger.

And the third brother, Philip, was a funny little kid, who really came out with some good one-liners. He was also the smart-mouthed little brother and the resident agitator, and he was good at it.

"Peter was always really particular about his collection of football cards," recalled Philip. "I was looking at his album of them one day, and he didn't want anyone else touching them and got really bent out of shape. He was trying to run into me with his wheelchair. So I positioned myself where he couldn't get to me, which made him even madder."

Looking back, Philip summarized.

"Back then, I always viewed Roger as kind of an unsuccessful experiment," said Philip, now thirty-seven. "I was really surprised you and Mom ever had any more kids at all. And then came Peter, and things got even worse. As I see it, I provided some comic relief, and was pretty much the glue that held everything together in those days."

Some things never change.

Quality(?) Time

It was my on-duty weekend. It had been a busy week at work, followed by a very active couple of days on call, and I was feeling pretty worn down, but also kind of guilty for not having spent much time with the boys lately. I finally got a break in the action in the middle of Sunday afternoon, so I asked them what they'd like to do.

"Can you watch the WWF with us?" all three asked in unison.

And why did I ask?

The WWF was short for the "World Wrestling Federation," which was the big show in pro wrestling in the '80s. It featured a madcap cavalcade of heroes and villains, each with his own goofy identity and shtick. The only thing "professional" about it was showmanship of these idiots, with the script for each match totally rigged. For any intelligent adult with half a brain, it was guaranteed to numb whatever half was there.

I always felt I probably should have been reported to Child Protective Services for letting them watch that kind of junk. But the WWF was hugely popular—one of the WWF's "Wrestle Mania" events had drawn a bigger crowd in Detroit than the pope—and our sons' friends and cousins all watched it, and so it happened that against our better judgment, our boys did too. And after walking into a trap of my own making, I was going to be watching an episode of the WWF.

In this particular installment, first, Randy "Macho Man" Savage beat the Honky Tonk Man. But then he got a guitar busted over his head while he was being held in the corner by the tag team of Jim "The Anvil," Brett "The Hitman," and their manager, Jimmy "Mouth of the South" Hart of the Hart Foundation. Macho Man's "manager," "the Lovely Elizabeth," was knocked down by Honky Tonk Man, and then someone went and got Hulk Hogan, who came to the rescue and straightened everything out.

Later, Hogan beat the Sheik, after he'd attempted to bite off a chicken's head.

So much for my efforts to spend "quality time" with my sons. The boys all absolutely ate this stuff up, and enjoyed my watching it with them. By the end of this unbridled stupidity, I wasn't sure I had a quarter of a brain left.

Whatever It Takes

I've always believed that one can learn something from most of his or her experiences, even the dumb ones. The WWF was no exception.

One day, after Peter's rough go of things in 1987, he was lying on the couch, trying to let his spinal fusion heal, and obviously not feeling well. In those days he and I played quite a bit of chess, but he really couldn't sit up to do that on this occasion. So I asked if there was anything else we could do together instead. A mischievous smile came over his face.

"Yeah. Can you beat up on Philip for me?" he mouthed.

Granted, a strange request by most standards, but if working over his pesky eight-year-old little brother—he wasn't known as "Phil the Pill" for nothing—would help Pete to feel better on this occasion, I figured it was the least I could do.

Philip had picked up on our conversation, and had taken off running. But I tackled him in the living room and threw him into a pile of floor pillows. Then I started using what I'd learned from the WWF. First I applied the dreaded "claw hold."

"Mom! Help! I'm getting killed!" he implored, but to no avail. She was no more inclined than Peter to come to his rescue. Note: For all of Philip's protests, he loved this stuff.

After I released him from the claw hold, then I applied a scissors hold, where I wrapped and locked my legs around his waist.

"Mom, help me!"

Then a scissors hold around his neck. By this time, Peter was beside himself laughing.

"Now can you do a 'pile driver' on him?" asked Pete.

"Sure. No problem."

In the WWF, a "pile driver" is when one wrestler picks up his opponent, and with the opponent's body totally upside down and vertical to the floor, drives his head and body directly into the mat. I'm not sure how they did pile drivers in the WWF without doing serious damage, but this was going to have to be a "modified" pile driver—we certainly didn't need two sons with serious spinal cord injuries. So for my grand finale, I did a "pile driver" on Philip, to Peter's exceeding delight. At that point, I was more afraid that Peter was going to rupture his spleen or something laughing than I was about Philip getting hurt, so I thought I'd better wrap this up.

I was pretty sure I'd made him feel better. Sometimes a dad's just got to do what a dad's got to do.

Bedtime Challenge

It didn't always seem like it at the time, but Sandra and I worked very well together as a team for Peter's care, and complemented each other nicely. She applied her excellent nursing skills, coordinated his care, kept things organized, handled all the details, and was a great mother. I did much of the "grunt work"—lifting Peter in and out of bed and elsewhere, dragging heavy oxygen tanks in and out of the house and Peter's room, lugging around cases of feeding and supplies, repairing wheelchairs and troubleshooting equipment, fighting with the insurance company, and helping her and taking my turn with routine medical care. I also figured it was part of my job to "keep things loose."

One night she'd gone to a meeting or something, and had laid down the law to Peter and me that he "absolutely" had to be in bed by eight sharp. No exceptions, no excuses, no nothing. He was tired, needed his rest, had a big day at school tomorrow, whatever.

We really did try. Peter's bedtime routine usually took at least an hour. But no matter how hard I tried to do Peter's care quickly and efficiently, I couldn't ever do it like she did. I could bust my tail hurrying, try every efficiency trick I could think of, and still not come within a half hour of matching her time for the same tasks. I don't know if it was stuff she learned in nursing school, part of being a woman's skill set, or just natural ability, but try as I might, I just couldn't measure up.

Anyway, on this occasion, I was busy and got started a little late. Then I knocked over one of Pete's medicine cups, which contained a sticky concoction, so I had to clean that up. We did watch a little of a football game that was on, but just a little.

By seven forty, it became obvious that we weren't going to meet our prescribed deadline, and I figured she was going to have a cow. Then I came up with this idea.

"Pete, let's get this finished up as fast as we can, and hope she doesn't come home until we get done," I said. "Then I'll act like we've been done for a long time. And do you think you can fake being asleep?"

He loved the idea! Eventually we did get done before she got home, but not by much. When she walked into his room, Peter tried to pretend he was in a deep slumber, but it's pretty hard to do when you're laughing. With Peter's love of fun and total inability to keep a straight face about much of anything, I should have known this half-baked scheme never had a chance.

Fortunately for us, Sandra got a kick out of it too, and forgot to get upset that we hadn't met our deadline.

CHAPTER 10
ON VACATION

Although Peter's multiple health problems presented us with many challenges, one of the things Sandra and I had decided early on was that we wanted to be as "normal" a family as we could under the circumstances. Part of that being "normal" included going on an occasional vacation.

Looking back, we would have liked to have gone on more trips, but Peter's hospitalizations and such precluded some of our plans. But we were able to go on some. And when we did, we had a great time.

Here are the stories of a few of them.

Lake Wawasee

One year when we came home from our annual vacation at Lake Wawasee, in northern Indiana, Peter said, "Could we just move to the lake? I'd like to live there all the time."

Going to the lake was something Sandra's parents started when she and her sisters and brother were kids, and it has continued as an annual week at the lake ever since, now into the fourth generation. It's no wonder that Peter and all of his cousins looked forward to the yearly excursion. Each family rents a cottage in the Oakwood Park section of the lake's west side, and for the whole week, people enjoy hanging out together at the beach, boating, skiing, swimming, playing board games, and more.

Some of Peter's favorite memories of the lake include the "Roscoe Buddies," a club for the boy cousins when they were young. Started by Uncle Randy, the club took its name from the *Dukes of Hazzard* TV show, which was popular at the time. No one else was ever invited to this annual meeting, but the boys had a blast eating pizza, watching a movie, and generally goofing off.

For several years, Dale Pence, a retired farmer and Purdue fan from near our home, would be vacationing at Oakwood Park on the same week we were there. A serious fisherman, he'd seen Peter in his Purdue cap and offered to take him fishing on his bass boat. I decided long ago that if I wanted to have fun, I wasn't going to depend on fish. I could never count on them to show up. But when we'd go out with Dale, I'd have to go along to help Peter get into the boat, and manage things for him while we were out.

I must have brought Dale my bad luck. Of all the years he took Peter and me out, I think Peter and Dale together only caught two or three fish worth keeping. But we had a good time. While we were waiting for the fish that invariably never showed up, we talked about Purdue sports, especially basketball. Everything from Coach Gene Keady's haircut, to the incoming recruits, to next year's prospects, to gossip about the inner workings of the team was fair game.

In more recent years, an annual feature of the week at the lake was the Fantasy Football draft. All of the male cousins, and by now cousins-in-law, had formed a Fantasy Football League. They'd make their selections, assemble their teams, then spend the next several months tracking their teams' fortunes, swapping players, and trash talking each other. The winner got his name mounted on a traveling plaque; the last-place finisher had to wear a dress at the next year's draft. Peter actually won the first championship, but never had to wear the dress. But win or lose, Peter lived for the Fantasy Football draft and the season that followed!

Of all the years we went to Lake Wawasee with Peter, what his medical situation was varied greatly from one year to another. Some years, for Peter, he was in relatively good shape. Other years, we had to set up a hospital bed in our cottage's living room to administer IVs and be able to care for some serious situation. Whatever his situation, we could always count on our extended family to pitch in and help us. Whether unloading a ton of medical supplies, or giving Sandra and I a break by getting Pete into or out of bed, they were there for us. They made it much easier for us to enjoy the week.

Another thing we enjoyed about going to the lake was an annual foray into northern Indiana's Amish Country, which was just about a half hour north of the lake. Going to the Das Dutchman's Essenhaus in Middlebury became an annual event for our immediate family. Even after Peter lost his ability to eat normally, he enjoyed going to the restaurant just to smell the delicious Amish cooking and pies, and be with the rest of us. In later years, when he was working, Peter would even pay for everyone's meal. We told him he didn't have to do that, but he insisted. Even though he couldn't enjoy the family-style dining himself, he enjoyed seeing us have a good time and getting to be a part of it so much that he said it was just something he wanted to do for us.

Washington, DC, 1988

We'd taken the boys to Florida and Disney World in 1985, and had planned to go on a "traveling vacation" every other year. But then 1987 happened, and Peter's care and condition escalated to a whole other level. For about the first year after 1987, we really didn't expect Peter to live very long. We didn't see how he could continue to go on with all of the serious challenges now impacting him. But he was hanging in there like the trouper he was, and making the best of his situation.

After a lot of discussion, Sandra and I decided to take the boys on a spring break trip to Washington DC. On one hand, we had a lot of apprehensions about taking Peter, in his condition and with all the work and logistics that would take. On the other hand, Roger was a junior in high school, and our window for such experiences with him was going to be closing rapidly. And if Peter really didn't have that much longer left, we thought it would be a fun experience and memories for him and all of us. I'd been to Washington several times before, and wanted the boys to have the experience of seeing the nation's capital and at least some of the cool things there. So somewhat against out better judgment, we decided to go for it. We figured in our case, going for "normal" sometimes included a few calculated risks.

The first thing we did was to rent a small U-Haul box trailer to pull behind our van to transport Peter's travelling ICU across parts of four states. We packed it with big oxygen tanks, ventilator, several cases of liquid feeding for Peter's feeding tube, boxes of medical supplies, Pete's wheelchair, some food for the rest of us, and our suitcases.

We didn't think that Peter could tolerate a trip of that length well sitting up, so he made the trip lying on the floor of the van on a gurney that someone had given us. In its collapsible state, it could also double as a cot for him once we got to Washington.

The trip out was an ordeal. We definitely wanted this to be a one-day trip, so we left very early on Friday morning and drove about thirteen hours, including through the mountains of Pennsylvania, to get there. All the way there, Peter never complained, despite his not being able to see anything on the outside from his vantage point on the floor. But he was in good spirits. At fairly regular intervals, he'd just hold his hand up for Sandra or I to "give him five," or smile at him.

We got to our hotel about 7:00 p.m. and immediately put Roger and Philip to work, starting to unload and move all the various supplies up to our room. I remember standing there in the parking lot of the hotel, unloading all of the stuff and feeling kind of embarrassed. If somebody was watching us, they had to be wondering what kind of traveling circus this was.

Once we got everything to our hotel room, we had to set up Peter's ventilator and other equipment, get the supplies arranged, and get everything operational. This took a few more hours, and by the time we finally got to bed, we were exhausted. But we'd made it!

The room was packed to the max, and we tripped over each other all week, but we made it work. Peter's gurney could be lowered and doubled as a cot for sleeping, but could be raised to where Sandra and I could work on him without having to ruin our backs. And despite my pre-vacation prediction that there was "no way we'd need a backup battery for Peter's ventilator," the hotel electricity did go out for a couple of hours during a storm one night. Fortunately Pete's ventilator's internal battery lasted that long.

We slept in on that Saturday morning, to try to recover some from our grueling day on Friday. Then we started seeing some of the many sights of Washington, DC, and the surrounding area. With Peter's situation and care, we were somewhat limited in what we could accomplish in a day. But we made it our goal to try to accomplish a "small day" of seeing things each day.

We made it a point to see many of the standard things in Washington, but also tried to take in a few things that were a little off the beaten path. Despite still being tired on Sunday morning, we dragged ourselves out of bed, got Peter up and going, and attended an Easter service at the National Cathedral. It was a perfect Sunday morning, and a brass ensemble filled the cathedral with music that was near-celestial.

Getting all of us seated with a wheelchair was a little challenging, but their ushers were great and made it happen. People were very nice and welcoming to us, even though we were dressed more casually than most of the people in the congregation. Afterward, we looked around some, and the boys thought it was too cool that there were people, including a former president, who were buried in the cathedral.

It was a great experience, and a great service. I've always been glad we made the effort to do that. And while we were in that neighborhood, we also went to the zoo, where Sandra enjoyed seeing the pandas.

Other excursions that were off the beaten path included Mount Vernon and the Naval Academy. One day, we even made the trip down to Colonial Williamsburg.

On the day we were going to try to see the White House, we got up early to try to "beat the crowd," but it didn't work. We'd been in line about an hour and a half, and it looked like we weren't going to make it in. Then from somewhere, Roger came up with this brochure that said for people in wheelchairs to go to a particular entrance. We asked a Secret Service man about it, and he said "sure," and personally took us there. When we went to Disney World in '85, Peter had gotten us to the front of many huge spring break lines. But now he'd gotten us into the White House! I guess it really is like they say in Washington; it's who you know!

Another day, we parked our van and took the subway from Alexandria, where we were staying, into the heart of DC. We spent the afternoon in the Smithsonian, and looked at the attractions along the National Mall and Reflecting Pool. In the evening, we saw the Lincoln Memorial, and were at the Vietnam Wall. I'd never seen it before, and it was sobering and overwhelming to see the names of all who lost their lives on the wall's panels. I'd just looked up a couple of my high school classmates whose names were on the wall, when Sandra alerted me that one of Peter's portable oxygen tanks had malfunctioned, and he now had no oxygen left.

We headed for the nearest subway entrance and got on as soon as we could. Since we were out of oxygen, she started using his emergency "ambu bag" to help him breathe and hopefully get some more oxygen. She was pretty scared, but Peter thought the whole thing was kind of funny.

The boys genuinely enjoyed the trip. As we'd walk different places, one time Roger jumped up on a pedestal and tried to "make like a statue," flexing his muscles like a WWF star. He was also good about helping us out by pushing Peter in his wheelchair. Philip was his normal pesky little brother self. Of course, there was the normal amount of the obligatory brotherly arguing and bickering. At one point, Peter said, "Dad, can you throw Philip in the Potomac for me?"

***

Looking back on that experience, it was a ton of planning and work, but it was worth it. We'd worried about Peter's physical condition and whether he could handle a trip like that. But our goal was always to shoot for as close to normal as we could, and he weathered it better than we ever would have guessed. I think the change of scenery actually did him some good. And during those times when the rest of us would be doing something he couldn't, like swimming in the hotel pool, he'd read a pro wrestling magazine or do something else to entertain himself. He just enjoyed being with us and doing something different, even if he couldn't participate fully.

We had a great time; the kids saw a lot and learned a lot, and it made a lasting impression. From that point on, whenever there was news on TV from Washington, one of the boys said "Oh, look … there's the Washington Monument, or Arlington National Cemetery, (or any number of other landmarks). We were there!"

Two memories that particularly stand out with the boys—they always remember the time we had to "help Peter breathe on the subway," and "the time we were at the Lincoln Memorial and Abe had a pigeon on his head."

Stadium Crashing

By the mid-'90s, Peter had regained enough strength, and Sandra and I had gotten better at managing his health needs, that we were able to take a few vacations at destinations within a day's drive. And although Peter couldn't do everything, he loved being with us and doing what he could. Once when we were at Grandfather Mountain in Western North Carolina, Philip and I tried to climb to the top. But Peter thoroughly enjoyed himself trying to see how many license plates from different states he could see down in the parking lot. Or while Philip and I went whitewater rafting, he and Sandra enjoyed just kicking back and watching movies.

One vacation activity particularly appealed to the boys. Football nut that I am, I like to stop in when I'm in the vicinity and visit some of the venerable stadiums from which I've seen many classic games on TV. I can't remember exactly when, but at some point I've thought it would be fun to actually "score" a touchdown or field goal in some of these hallowed places. So when no one's looking, I just kind of wander out on the field with my football and indulge my Walter Mitty fantasies of what could have been but, unfortunately, never was.

As the boys have gotten into this, one of us may crash across the goal line against an imaginary defense stacked against us. Or make a Sports

Center Top Ten catch in the corner of the end zone. Or I may kick a game-winning field goal as time expires. I may even attempt a "Lambeau Leap!" Then, forever after, when we see one of these venues on TV, we always tell whoever else is watching, "I've scored in that end zone!"

It's great fun while it lasts, but, almost invariably, some stadium employee sees these goings-on, and we get the boot. Some are reasonably good natured about it, some much less so. But by the time they bid us a not-so-fond farewell, we've scored at Lambeau Field (Green Bay), at Notre Dame, at Soldier Field (Chicago). The list goes on. That has become part of the game, to see how many points we can score before the "clock runs out."

When we've been on vacations, we've been able to enjoy some great father-and-son bonding time (now being passed down to my grandsons!) participating in these stealth activities. Occasionally, we don't even get kicked out. At Wake Forest and Appalachian State, we were able to play joyfully for the better part of a whole quarter, uninterrupted!

Peter tended to fare better than the rest of us in these events. On another occasion I had him at Soldier Field throwing him passes in the end zone, and the stadium manager came our way. I thought to myself, *I know where this is going.* Instead, he gave Peter his business card and said to call him if we'd ever like to go to a game!

One time was particularly memorable. In '97, we were on a week's vacation in the Smoky Mountains, and Peter, Philip and I drove over to the University of Tennessee to make a little history there. That was in June, and on that particular occasion, a Promise Keepers group was setting up for one of their events.

That time all we had was a nerf football, but I was throwing some touchdown passes to Peter and Phil in the end zone when a Promise Keeper approached us.

"I'm sorry, fellas, but you're really not supposed to be here," he said, almost embarrassed. "I really hate to do this, but I'm going to have to ask you to leave. I really am sorry."

As we left, Peter said, "Boy, Dad, that's the politest we've ever been kicked out. Those Promise Keepers are really nice guys."

CHAPTER 11
OF DOCTORS, NURSES, AND MARY POPPINS

Over the course of Peter's life, we've lost count of how many doctors Peter had, consulted with, or were seen by at some point or other, but there were many.

We were blessed to have primary doctors who were excellent physicians in each of their specialties. But they were much more than that. They were even better human beings. To them, Peter wasn't just a patient. They cared as much, if not more, about him as a person. And so too with Sandra and me.

Stories and jokes about doctors who "think they're God" abound. We encountered a few of those types along the way but didn't stay with them long. The doctors we worked with long term didn't see themselves as God, but considered themselves honored to be able to assist him in the healing process.

When we saw them, it wasn't just an office visit. They had become our friends.

There were too many to mention everyone in this book. But here are just a few of them.

Dr. Henry Feuer

We met Dr. Feuer very soon after Peter was born. A handsome and likable young neurosurgeon on the staff at Riley Hospital, he closed the opening in Peter's back the day he was born. Then a few days later, he implanted a shunt in the lower right portion of Peter's head to drain off the excess spinal fluid from his brain caused by hydrocephalus.

A few years later, Dr. Feuer moved to a private practice, Indianapolis Neurosurgical Group, at Methodist Hospital, and all of Peter's neurosurgical care followed him there. One time we were seeing him in his office and noticed that his bachelor's degree was from the University of Maryland, and Peter and I asked him about being a "Terrapin." I forget exactly what he said about that, but it was obvious that he could relate to our sports-related questions.

A few years after that, Peter's case was transferred to Dr. Michael Turner, who had been a student of Dr. Feuer at the IU Med Center, and was now Indianapolis Neurosurgical's new pediatric neurosurgery specialist. But when Dr. Turner was tied up or away, we'd still see Dr. Feuer for routine visits.

In 1980, we were surprised to see Dr. Feuer's name turn up in a story in *Sports Illustrated.* He had performed a successful surgery—considered ground-breaking at the time—on an Indiana University basketball star, Mike Woodson. Dr. Feuer had removed a disk from between two of Woodson's vertebrae, alleviating his serious back problems. Woodson was back playing Big Ten basketball again in seven weeks, which was unheard of then.

Dr. Feuer was also the only doctor who hadn't been fired by IU coach Bobby Knight in his quest to find a cure for Woodson's nagging back issues. This may have been his bigger accomplishment.

When we mentioned seeing the article to Dr. Feuer, he characteristically downplayed it.

"Thanks. It was a nice article, but now I'm getting calls from all over the country from people who think I'm some miracle doctor who can cure all of their back ailments. I really kind of wish that article would just go away."

When the NFL's Baltimore Colts moved to Indianapolis in 1984, we soon began to see Dr. Feuer on their sidelines as the neurosurgical consultant to the team. He continued in that role for decades, even after retiring from his regular practice.

Whenever Peter would see Dr. Turner, we'd get updates on Dr. Feuer and the Colts. At one point, he'd apparently gotten his leg broken when a player crashed into him out of bounds. But he also received a Super Bowl ring when the Colts won Super Bowl XLI.

Years later, I heard former Colts' GM Bill Polian, now an ESPN analyst, discussing Peyton Manning's neck situation on *Sports Center*.

"The Colts have the best neurosurgeon in Hank Feuer in the United States, if not the world," he said. "If Dr. Feuer says Manning's neck is okay, then it's okay."

To this day, whenever any of us see Dr. Feuer on the Colts' sideline, we say, "We know him!"

Dr. Michael Turner

When we were first told that Peter's case was going to be switched from Dr. Feuer to Dr. Turner, who was the practice's new pediatric neurosurgery specialist, we were all kind of bummed out. We really liked Dr. Feuer and didn't want to switch.

But Dr. Turner quickly "grew on us." He had a positive, upbeat nature about him that all of us could easily relate to. He'd come into the exam room and say things like, "I've reviewed the CT scans of your brain, and I've got good news, Peter—you still have a brain."

He was a good neurosurgeon. He was conservative, not prone to rush into aggressive interventions until the time was right. But when action was called for, he'd get right on it. He was there with us through some of our most difficult times, over a period of nearly thirty years. When we first met him, he was the "young guy" in the practice. The last time we saw him, he was getting ready to retire.

He was one of those doctors we trusted, and felt very comfortable working with. And he felt very comfortable with us and confident in our abilities as parents, particularly Sandra and her nursing skills. One time I overheard him and Peter's infectious doctor at the time, Dr. Karen Israel, having a discussion over whether to bring Peter back into the hospital or not. Dr. Israel wanted to, Dr. Turner didn't.

"For most things, Peter gets better care at home than we can give him here," he told her.

Dr. Richard Lindseth

Dr. Lindseth was Peter's longtime orthopedic doctor. We knew he was nationally recognized for his work with spina bifida kids and bracing, and a strong advocate for kids and families affected by spina bifida. But during an office visit in 1987, we learned that he'd been invited to China for a month to consult with doctors working with kids with spina bifida there.

"Any chance you could use Peter and us as 'demonstrators' or 'case studies' on your trip?" I asked.

"Probably not," he laughed. "But I really appreciate your offer."

Next time we saw him, I asked about his China trip. I found the whole thing fascinating, and wanted to learn more. He was more than happy to oblige me, talking about it for a good twenty minutes.

Afterward, Peter, who had no particular interest in international medicine or politics, said "Thanks a lot, Dad. I wasn't really dying to hear all of that."

Dr. Lindseth went on more trips. The next time I asked him again, partly because I was interested, partly because I knew I could agitate Peter by doing so. As Dr. Lindseth went on at length, I could see Peter out of the corner of my eye. He was being very polite, but gave me a look which I recognized as, "Will you please just shut up? Enough, already."

But of all the time we spent with Dr. Lindseth, the memory that sticks out most to me was in 1984, when Peter was in Methodist Hospital with meningitis. Once when someone was there visiting, Sandra borrowed their car and made the short trip from Methodist to Riley to see Dr. Lindseth about something. She told him what had been happening with Peter, and tears started rolling down his cheeks.

We knew that Dr. Lindseth was a physician who cared deeply about his young patients. But that spontaneous demonstration of empathy really touched Sandra and me. We were blessed.

Dr. Susan Maisel

We first met Dr. Maisel when she consulted with Peter for gastroenterological matters at Methodist Hospital. Later she moved over to St. Vincent's Hospital on Indianapolis's northwest side, and we followed her there.

An excellent doctor, she also became a friend. Later on, much of the time it was just Peter and I taking a lot of the doctor trips when we'd see her. Somehow it came up in the conversation that one of her neighbors was Peyton Manning. She said she never saw him, but that she knew he lived there. Every time after that, we'd always ask about her "famous neighbor."

One time she shared with us that another of her patients who also had a J-tube had been celebrating his twenty-first birthday. One of his brothers had poured beer into his J-tube, and he'd wound up in the ER.

"Peter, I'll tell you right now, if you ever pull a stunt like that, you won't have to worry about going to the ER. I'll strangle you myself," she said with a laugh.

Whenever we were there, she'd always ask about Sandra and the rest of our family, and would send her best wishes. Then she'd always give us a hug before we left.

Undoubtedly one of Dr. Maisel's biggest contributions to Peter's care was to come years after. More about that later.

Dr. Joe Hannah

Dr. Hannah had been Peter's pediatrician forever. But when Peter became an adult, we ran into a dilemma. Peter was of the first generation of kids with spina bifida to have lived into adulthood in any numbers, and adult doctors didn't know what to do with them.

As we discussed this with Dr. Hannah, he told us that we probably needed to consider an adult physician at some point, but he was quite willing to continue with Peter in the meantime. He also really didn't know what adult doctor would be willing to take on a case of Peter's complexity. We told him that if he didn't mind, we'd be glad to continue with him.

"I'm okay with that," he smiled. "Peter's probably my all-time favorite patient, and if you can put up with me, I'll be glad to keep him as my patient." So Peter continued to see Dr. Hannah well into his thirties.

Whenever we'd see Dr. Hannah, we'd always cover the medical stuff, but would wind up talking about any number of other topics. Dr. Hannah loved to do photography and had become an accomplished amateur digital photographer. There was a nicely framed and matted image on his wall of a strikingly beautiful tiger that he'd photographed at the Indianapolis Zoo.

"That's so cool," said Peter. "I just love tigers, and that's one of the best pictures of one I've ever seen."

Appointment over, we were out in the parking lot getting loaded up in the van when I saw Dr. Hannah walking toward us carrying something.

"Peter, I'd be honored for you to have this picture," he told Peter. It was the framed photo of the tiger we'd just finished discussing.

Both Peter and I were speechless. Each of us finally got out a "thank you," but it seemed so inadequate. Over the years I'd learned to gracefully accept gifts of love from others, but I relapsed. I couldn't resist saying, "You really don't need to do that."

"That's okay," he said. "I'm glad to do that for Peter. I think he might enjoy it even more than me."

Dr. Michael Tsangaris

I forget when I first met Dr. Tsangaris. By this time, Sandra's and my roles had done something of a switch, with my schedule being more flexible than hers, and I wound up doing many of the doctor trips. She just told me that he was Peter's new pulmonologist, and that his appointment was at three thirty at Riley/IU North Hospital.

And like Dr. Hannah, Dr. Tsangaris was a *pediatric* pulmonary physician. Again, with adult doctors not having much, if any, experience with the first generation of kids with spina bifida to live into adulthood, it just made sense for him to continue to follow Peter, even as he became an adult.

The first time I met him, he seemed like a nice enough guy, but I really didn't think too much about it. I just wanted to get the day finished and get going. But I did notice that he seemed to spend ample time with Peter, and was very thorough.

But over the years we all got to know him much better, as he did us. When I'd take Peter down for an appointment, Dr. Tsangaris and Peter would spend the first fifteen or twenty minutes discussing Peter's medical stuff. Then the conversation would shift. Invariably to sports. They'd talk for another fifteen or twenty about Purdue or IU basketball, sometimes Butler basketball, sometimes the NFL. He and Peter would laugh, joke, and swap ideas on how each of those sports entities could do better.

At first, I was amazed at how much time Dr. Tsangaris spent with us. But as I observed these goings-on, there was clearly something different. It wasn't doctor to patient. It was friend to friend. They clearly enjoyed each other's company, and they both looked forward to these visits.

"It was really, really fun for me, and I always enjoyed Peter's visits," said Dr. Tsangaris. "And I really admired Peter. He had more complications than anybody else would have had in a hundred lifetimes. But he was always upbeat, had a smile, and was an inspiration to me."

Over time, Sandra and I also became friends with Dr. Tsangaris. He called each of us by our first names, and we could just tell that he liked us, and we him. One time when Peter was a patient at Riley/

IU North, I was staying with Pete and got up early for breakfast. Dr. Tsangaris came over and joined me, asked how we were getting along with this extended stay, and was very genuine.

I'd never had that happen before, a doctor joining me for breakfast. It was so different. But with Dr. Tsangaris, it felt so normal.

Nurses

While it's the doctors who call the shots, it's the nurses who give them—and a whole lot more. Over the years, Peter had literally hundreds of different nurses during his countless hospital stays. Most were good, but we were blessed to have a good number who were excellent.

On one hand, Peter never liked going into the hospital. But from the time he was an infant, going there on a pretty regular basis was just a normal part of life for him. So in typical Peter fashion, he'd just make the best of it. The great majority of Peter's hospitalizations were in either pediatric units or pediatric intensive care units, even after he became an adult. And people person that he was, there was a large part of him that enjoyed the socializing that would come with it. And it wasn't just limited to nurses. Respiratory therapists, "playroom ladies," custodians, and more, all got to be friends with Peter.

From about 1990 through 1995, Peter was in Riley Hospital and the Methodist Pediatric Units a lot. It was at about that time that he first met Rene Cain at the Methodist Pediatric ICU. Rene worked as part of a team with two other nurses, Amy Rowland and Claudia Moran. All three took turns taking care of Peter, and Peter was in the hospital so much that we all got to know them very well. For years, we'd heard comments about nurses competing to see "who got to take care of Peter that day."

"It was true," said Rene. "There really was a friendly rivalry. Nurses did enjoy the opportunity to take care of him. He really had kind of a 'magnetic personality,'" and was highly social. He was always so upbeat and positive, and glad to see us. And there were so many times that he was in pretty bad shape, really didn't feel good, and had so much going on that it would be normal to complain about. But I never, ever heard him complain."

And in a pediatric ICU, there was very much of a family atmosphere. As the nurses would take care of Pete, there would be nonstop conversations (during this time, Peter couldn't talk, and they were all pretty good at reading his lips) about a huge range of topics. They knew that Peter was a Purdue fan, and the great majority of nurses were either IU grads or had some IU connections, so that was a never-ending source of jokes, teasing, and back and forth. And many of Peter's hospitalizations were long enough that we got to know about their families, and they, ours. Once, after Peter was home, Rene and Claudia came up from Indianapolis to our house to visit, and Sandra took them over to see her horse, Lady.

Amy and Claudia later moved out of state. But Rene continued to "just show up" during a number of Peter's hospitalizations over a period of about twenty-five years. Wherever they were, they always stayed in contact.

"For me, it was always an honor and a privilege to be able to take care of Peter," said Rene. "He became like a brother to me. And he inspired me, to be a better nurse, and a better person."

The flip side of that was that not only Rene, Claudia, and Amy, but many, many nurses over the years inspired us. Not only did they provide excellent, beyond-the-call-of-duty-type care that helped keep him alive and able to live as normal a life as possible, they did much more. They became friends to Peter and us, and played no small part in helping to keep us all sane and make difficult situations fun.

God bless 'em.

Mary Poppins Was Right

All of Peter's specialists were in Indianapolis. Whenever it was time for appointments, Sandra was a master at being able to cram multiple doctor visits into one day. Almost always we'd have at least two, usually three, and when we could work in four, it was kind of a grand slam.

Although we saved a lot of time—and time on the road—by doing so, those were grueling days. We'd usually have to leave early in the morning, spend two hours on the road, run all over downtown Indy, try to keep on schedule, help Peter "pull maintenance," try to squeeze in a meal, and spend hours waiting in offices or hospitals. Then two hours back home. Often we'd get home well into the evening.

One thing we came up with early on was to try to do some fun activity of some sort when the doctor visits were over. Often this consisted of some shopping at one of Indy's malls, a meal at a nice restaurant, visiting the Eiteljorg Museum of Indians and Western Art, an Indianapolis Indians baseball game, or something else of interest.

Mary Poppins used to say that "A spoonful of sugar helps the medicine go down," and she was right! Just having something to look forward to at the end of the day, and being able to finish on a fun note, made a world of difference in making those long days bearable.

We did lots of different things for our "fun activities." But here are a few that stick out in my memory.

***

One time, when Peter would have been about twelve, we'd wrapped up the schedule of doctor visits, and Pete and I were waiting on Sandra to finish up something. So I asked Peter what he'd like to do on the way home that day.

"Why don't we eat at Fazoli's?" he said. "I'd really like to do that."

Fazoli's? That one totally threw me. Here's a kid that can't eat regular food, takes all his nourishment by a feeding tube, and he wants to go to Fazoli's for fun? I pondered this for a moment, then finally had to dig a little deeper.

"Pete," I started out somewhat hesitantly, "Fazoli's is a good place, but you can't eat. Of all the things we could do, why would you want to go to Fazoli's for our fun activity?"

"I just love it there," he said. "Everything there just smells so good."

***

On another occasion later that year, we went shopping at Lafayette

Square mall, on Indy's near west side. As Peter and I made our way down one of the corridors, a nice-looking, athletic young man saw Peter and made a beeline over to say "Hi."

That was during the years that Peter couldn't talk normally, but whoever this personable guy was, he could obviously read Peter's lips very well. They launched into their conversation so quickly and enthusiastically that Peter never thought about introducing me, and I saw no point in interrupting.

Early in their discussion I figured out that this was an Indianapolis Colt, as he and Peter chatted away like old friends about off-season workouts, picking up free agents, and the prospects for next season. He was very gracious and appeared to be enjoying the conversation just as much as Peter. After about ten minutes, he told Peter, "Good to see you, Pete, but I need to get going; take care, buddy," and moved on.

By now, my curiosity was going bonkers.

"So who was that?" I asked.

"Oh, that was Dean Biasucci (Colts placekicker who'd been named as a Pro Bowl and All-Pro selection earlier that year). I got to know him when I was in the hospital."

***

Another time, Peter was now somewhere in his twenties and it was just him and me in Indianapolis for a rare single doctor visit. We were done by early afternoon and had some extra time on our hands. As we were getting ready to leave the parking lot, Peter caught me off guard.

"Hey Dad. Since Mom's not here today and it's just you and me, for our fun activity of the day, how about if we go to Hooters?"

I had a good laugh, but we didn't go to Hooters. I suspected his interest was in more than just "the way the food smells there."

CHAPTER 12
MOVING ON

With elementary school behind him, Peter, Sandra, and I started looking ahead to junior high. We'd been so busy dealing with his various medical crises, trying to do our jobs as best we could and meet the needs of two other sons that the time had passed quickly. For Peter, the junior high and early high school period turned out to be a time of continuing and escalating medical conditions, coupled with the opportunities that came with becoming a "normal" teenager.

Rambo Delivers

The summer before he started seventh grade, in 1988, Peter would be in his fourth year of 4-H. So far, he'd mainly taken pigs as his project, and Roger had taken care of them and shown them for him. But this year, Sandra wanted to try something different. She thought rabbits would be a good project for Peter, and had heard about someone she thought could help.

So we made an appointment with Mr. Don Weaver, a local gentleman who loved rabbits and was really into showing them. Almost immediately, Mr. Weaver took a liking to Peter, and made a point to pick out some good ones for him. Peter came home with two rabbits—a brown Castor Rex and a Florida White. Peter named the white one

Rambo, after the Sylvester Stallone ultimate action hero who was the hottest thing in movies at the time. In an address to the nation on some national security issue, President Reagan had once said he "wished he could call on Rambo for this mission."

We'd gotten a rabbit hutch somewhere, and Sandra drafted Roger to help her build a runway of patio blocks for Peter to be able to get his wheelchair out to tend his rabbits. He really got into it! He spent many hours during the summer feeding, petting, and working with them. Mr. Weaver had told Peter to feed them a raisin or two every day, as that would be good for their coats, and Peter did it faithfully.

When the fair came, Peter was getting ready for the rabbit show, and I told Pete we needed to have a "pep talk" with Rambo before the show.

"Rambo, look at me. Peter and I have a mission for you. Your job is to go into that show ring with those 170 other rabbits, and bring out the hardware. Got it?"

Rambo never answered, just wiggled his nose. But Peter loved it.

The show began. Rambo won the first class he was in, and then got a trophy for being the champion junior buck. Then another for the champion fancy rabbit. As the show continued on well into the evening, Rambo was still in contention. When they finally had the best-of-show competition, Rambo was named grand champion of the whole show!

The fair queen presented Peter the trophy, a reporter from the *Wabash Plain Dealer* interviewed me for Peter, and the photographer took his picture with the queen and trophy. The next day's paper included a very nice article about Peter and Rambo. Lots of people came up to congratulate Pete. A couple of weeks later, we took Rambo to the state fair, where in much stiffer competition he did well there too, winning a blue ribbon.

Sylvester Stallone himself couldn't have accomplished the "mission" any better.

Sandra was a lot more enthusiastic about rabbits than I was. I was primarily a "pig guy," who didn't know a champion rabbit from a jackrabbit. But as was often the case, she was right. It had been a great project and a great experience for Peter.

High Price of Pork

On Friday night of that week was the 4-H auction, where local merchants and business people buy the kids' animals. Peter didn't sell Rambo, since he'd decided to take him to the state fair, but did sell his pig. When the time came for Peter's pig to sell, Roger was selling it for him, and I scooted Peter's wheelchair as close to the auction ring as I could, so the bidders could hopefully better recognize that the pig was actually Peter's.

Our family physician, Dr. Haughn, almost always bought our kids' pigs, and they typically sold pretty well. This year, the average price was around $1.25 per pound. But when the bidding commenced, it started at a dollar, then two, then three, then four … and kept going. I couldn't believe it; I was in a state of shock! So was Peter. When the bidding finally stopped, Peter had received $7.50 a pound, even more than the grand champion!

Turned out that a group of farmers from our church had teamed up with Dr. Haughn, all under the umbrella of "Friends of Peter Boone" to buy Peter's pig, since he wasn't selling Rambo. The crowd gave him a big hand, and Peter waved to them. Afterward, many people came up and congratulated him—several farmers telling him, "I wish I could sell hogs like that."

When Peter got his nice check for $1,725 a few days later, Peter gave $100 of it to the church and $100 to the fair's building fund.

For any 4-H'er, winning best of show in any project is a big thrill. But there was something about this that was especially sweet. After all Peter had been through the past couple of years, it felt so good to see him having fun, learning responsibility, experiencing some success, and getting a little recognition from some normal activities.

***

Roger sold his pig immediately after Peter's. After a slow start, Roger's sold for $1.60. On one hand, a really good price, compared to the average. On the other, a far cry from his brother's $7.50. As good as I felt for Peter, I really felt bad for Roger. He was a good kid who did much of the work, but still frequently wound up in Peter's shadow. I talked with Peter, and we wound up giving him $100 from Peter's check.

Starting Junior High

It didn't seem possible that it was time for Peter to be going to junior high. After our initial apprehensions, Southwood Elementary had been a wonderful, very warm, and comfortable experience, and we were somewhat spoiled.

But junior high? Again, we were feeling apprehensive. When Peter had started at Southwood Elementary, he had some physical issues, but things looked reasonably normal, and the "big stuff" came later, after everyone already knew him. At Southwood Junior-Senior High School, he would largely be starting over, now be one of the "little kids," and one who couldn't talk and had a wheelchair loaded down with oxygen tanks and suction machine to boot. Would the older kids accept him? Would the administrators be as welcoming and helpful as Mr. Arnold? Here he'd have more teachers than in elementary school. Would they love Peter as much as the ones at SES?

Sometime before school started, we made an appointment with the new principal, Mr. Mitchell, and Sandra, Peter, and I went down to meet him. When we got there, we also met Mr. Dawson, who was the new assistant principal. We just introduced ourselves and Peter to them, told them a little about Peter, and gave them copies of our annual "handout."

Then we just asked a few questions about bathroom facilities, getting him a shelf in his locker—which was a new experience—so he could reach his books from his wheelchair, and getting a desk sized for him in each of his rooms.

Both Mr. Mitchell and Mr. Dawson were Purdue grads, which impressed Peter, and when they found out that he was a Purdue fan, both took a quick liking to him. We did a quick tour of the building, checked out Peter's new locker-to-be, then told them we'd see them when school started. They seemed nice enough, and it had been a good visit, and Sandra, Peter, and I were feeling about as comfortable as we could. But years later, Mr. Mitchell confided to Sandra that he and Mr. Dawson had been even more apprehensive than we were.

"We were sweating it," he said. "We'd heard that this kid who couldn't talk and who has all kinds of medical complications was coming, and we'd never experienced anything even remotely like that before. But you were all so nice. You never made a bunch of demands, you just asked some good questions, and mostly just said, 'What can we do to help you and the teachers?'"

***

It was hard seeing him go up the ramp and into the junior-senior high school building the first time, the first student who had ever come there in a wheelchair. But despite some early days where he didn't feel that good, or had headaches, we were really surprised at how readily he seemed to adapt.

I'd seen him at some social situation around that time where he really didn't know that many people, and it was really interesting. Rather than being some shrinking violet that was self-conscious about his inability to talk, or having to suction occasionally, Peter would go up and "talk" confidently with anybody! He had no fear! And for the most part, he seemed to be able to make people understand him, and they enjoyed talking with him. I figured that was probably pretty much what was taking place at school.

Sandra still worried about him adapting, and one day after about a month, she asked Roger, who was a senior, and center on the varsity football team, if he'd ever seen or heard anything about any of the students making fun of Peter. He assured her that he not only hadn't, but didn't anticipate it likely ever happening.

"If anyone ever did make fun of him, I'm sure E. J. and Brad (two of his larger defensive lineman teammates) would have a very serious talk with them."

Peter Joins the Football Team

Just a few days into the school year, I went to school at three thirty and sought out Mr. Wente, the seventh-grade football coach. I just told him a little about Peter and how much he loved sports, and asked if there was anything he could do to help out with the team. He was in a hurry to get to practice, but said, "Sure, that would be great. We can have him keep stats at the games or something."

That sounded like great news to Peter, who was ecstatic. Peter just had to go to the games, not practice, which worked out well with his physical situation. But we went down to watch a practice or two, just to familiarize. Peter loved being there and feeling like he was going to be part of the action. I was also impressed with his ability to recognize formations. He'd watched enough football on TV that he could readily identify whether teams were running a 5–2 or a 4–4 defense, or an I formation or split backfield. As we watched, he got even more enthused, and over the season his love for football grew stronger than ever. He'd talked about it constantly.

"Hey Dad. Do you know what I think would be really cool? I'd love to be a wishbone quarterback, like at Oklahoma. I think it would be so much fun to direct a triple-option attack."

Soon the first game came. Peter was keeping the tackle charts for the seventh- and eighth-grade teams, and I became his "spotter." By standing, I had a much better vantage point than he did sitting in his wheelchair, so I'd see who made the tackle, and then relay that to Peter, who would record it on his clipboard.

By the end of the first quarter, Peter was comfortable with his new duties, and having a blast. And frankly, so was I. I hadn't been on a football sideline since my White's coaching days, and had missed it greatly. It was so great to "be back." But it was even greater to be there with Peter. Just to see him being at least some part of an athletic team choked me up. I couldn't have been prouder of him if he'd scored eight touchdowns.

At one point during the first game, the tacklers pursued their prey out of bounds and landed pretty close to us.

"You'd better be careful," I told Peter. "If anyone winds up injuring themselves on your wheelchair, you'll get flagged for unnecessary roughness," which cracked him up.

In another of the earlier games, Southwood was playing a team from Huntington, and our eighth grade wound up handling theirs 46–6.

"Pete, get ready to go in," said Mr. Wente. "We've subbed so much that you're the only one left who hasn't been in the game yet," which delighted Peter no end. After the game, the eighth-grade players doused their coach, Mr. Livergood, with water from the Gatorade container, which Peter thought was too cool.

The players were great about making Peter feel a part of things. Although it wasn't realistic for them to have extended conversations with him on the sidelines, there was always something like, "Hey, Pete, how you doing?" or "Hey, Pete, did you see my tackle?" or "Hey, Pete, you're dragging a hose,"—most likely from his suction machine. And it didn't appear to me that they were "just trying to be nice." They genuinely liked him, respected him, and were glad to have him as a part of their team.

Peter was loving it. If he'd have been in heaven, I'm not sure he could have been any happier.

**

Pretty quickly after Peter started seventh grade, he joined our church's youth group, which he enjoyed immensely. And first chance he had, he also joined the Southwood huddle of the Fellowship of Christian Athletes. While he wasn't an "athlete" in the truest definition of the word, he was a member of an athletic team, which apparently met the requirements. In any case, he was met with open arms by both groups.

Peter had always been involved in church and Sunday school. But both of these groups were voluntary, and he joined them as quickly as he could. He attended both as often as conditions would permit. And from both groups, he found a niche where he enjoyed the acceptance, friendship, and the spiritual growth opportunities that each afforded.

**

As it turned out, for the next three years, for both football and basketball, whenever he was able, Peter was the statistician for his grade's teams. And I was his transporter and spotter. Whoever was the coach of the team also became Peter's "coach." I could fill a whole chapter with just stories about those days, but here are just a few of them.

Of Stats, Jokes, and Translators

Peter had Mr. Grinstead for his general science class. Roger had had him for advanced biology and said that while he was a good teacher, he wasn't an easy one, and we wondered how that would work. But Mr. Grinstead was an avid Purdue fan, and he took a real liking to Peter, and Peter enjoyed his class. One day at about the end of the junior high football season, he made Peter's day.

"Hey Dad. Guess what. Mr. Grinstead asked me to be his statistician for the seventh-grade basketball team!"

"So what did you tell him?"

He gave me this look, like "What do you *think* I told him?"

So Peter and I started keeping stats for the Southwood seventh-grade basketball team. There was more to keep track of in basketball—rebounds, assists, shot chart, turnovers—it was faster paced than football, and Peter's fine motor skills weren't the best. So I needed to be on top of my game, to be able to relay everything correctly for Peter to record.

Besides Peter getting to be a part of the team, he and I were having a lot of fun. One day at a tournament in Logansport, he was giggling about something, and I asked him what was up. He told me he'd been keeping "stats on my jokes," and so far, I wasn't having a good day. By his count, I'd supposedly made seven bad jokes to only one good one. I kidded him that he was supposed to be keeping stats on the game, not my jokes. And besides that, I hoped he was doing a whole lot better job on the former than the latter!

After the kids had gotten out of the showers following the games, they'd come rushing up to Peter, one after another.

"How many rebounds did I get, Pete?" or "How many points did I score, Pete?" or "I had three assists, and you've only got me down for two, Pete."

The team was also very good, losing only a game or two the whole season. That core group of players—Mike Wilhelm, David Rigney, Ben Speicher, Isaac Winer, David Wiley, Christian Perry, and twins Dick and Doug Smith, stayed together throughout all of their junior high and high school days, and were good friends of Peter's. David Rigney was one of Peter's better friends. Years later I bumped into Mr. Grinstead while we were waiting for our cars to get serviced, and he shared some reminiscences with me.

"David and Pete were two of my all-time favorite boys; I loved those kids," he said. "When Pete became our statistician, I couldn't read his lips. I really tried, but I just couldn't do it. But David could do it real well. So when I needed to talk with Pete, I'd just call David in, and he'd be my interpreter. We wound up having some great three-way conversations. It was one of the coolest things I've ever experienced."

Hangin' Out With Cousin Eddie

Once Peter started being a statistician, he never had a problem "finding work." For his eighth-grade year, David's dad, Tom Rigney, was an elementary principal and the eighth-grade basketball coach. He had "seen Peter in action," in the seventh grade and early on recruited a very willing Peter to keep stats for him too.

The eighth-grade basketball team continued to be as successful as they'd been in seventh grade, and everyone was having fun. Mr. Rigney also seemed to really have a heart for Peter, and did everything in his power to make him feel a part of things. During Christmas break, he decided he wanted to do some kind of team activity, and thought about taking them to a movie.

The way the story came down to me through Peter was that apparently Mr. Rigney had asked David what movie he thought the guys would like to see. David told him that Peter said he'd seen an advertisement for this one new movie, *Christmas Vacation*, where the cat gets electrocuted or something, and thought that looked pretty good. So Mr. Rigney arranged for a team movie a few days after Christmas. I took Peter in our van and followed the team bus to Marion.

I wound up sitting next to Mr. Rigney, and Peter sat next to me in the theater aisle. Not long into the movie, it became apparent that this probably hadn't been a good choice. It was rated PG-13, which was about the age of the boys, but it was an edgy PG-13, pushing the limits of that rating. I was under no illusions that all of the boys hadn't seen similar things before, but as a school-sponsored activity, it really wasn't appropriate, which was kind of awkward.

But it was funny! Throughout the movie, I was torn between feeling bad for Mr. Rigney and fearing I was going to laugh myself to death. It was the funniest movie I'd ever seen. Peter and I laughed till we cried.

As years passed, Christmas Vacation became an annual ritual for our family, except for Sandra, who thought it was stupid—women frequently have no taste when it comes to great movies—but Peter and I couldn't wait to watch it every Christmas season. We became like the two proverbial long-term convicts, who laughed at their old jokes just by the number. All I'd have to say to Peter was "Hey, look kids—a deer," or "We're going to have the hap, hap, happiest Christmas since ..." and Peter would be laughing himself silly. But for all the times we've watched that movie, we were in total agreement—there was no time like the first!

***

Mr. Wente was the freshman basketball coach. Early in the season, I was helping Peter keep stats at Manchester, and we were sitting pretty close to Mr. Wente, who was a pretty funny guy, and we discovered that he talked to himself a lot during the games. At one point, as the official ran past him, he said, "You have definite visual problems" a little too loudly, whereupon the ref promptly stopped and whistled him for a technical foul. Peter and I tried not to be too obvious about laughing at his predicament, but weren't all that successful.

Peter missed the last part of the freshman season, being in the hospital for several weeks for a surgery during which they installed his colostomy. At one point during that stretch, I stopped down at Southwood High School to pick up some college financial aid forms for

Roger. As I was leaving, Mr. Wente saw me in the hallway and asked how Peter was doing.

Then he told me how the freshman team had won their tourney, but the players had all worn black shoes during the game to honor Peter. To break their huddles at time-outs, instead of "team" they'd say "Peter." During the trophy presentation, the team had been chanting, "Peter."

"It was pretty touching," he said. "For kids of this age, it's really unusual for them to take that much of an interest in someone else."

Following the season, at the athletic banquet, when Coach Wente was wrapping his part of the presentation, he said that this year they had an unprecedented, special "MVP" award. He said that this recipient wasn't a player, so he couldn't be named most valuable player, so they created something new—a "most valuable person" award—for Peter.

He got a standing ovation. I got tears.

***

His freshman year was the last time Peter ever kept any stats. For as much as he loved it, being on the sidelines during high school varsity football games could be hazardous, for both Peter and players who might crash into his wheelchair. And in basketball, moving up to a varsity commitment, with all of the additional time and travel required was more than Peter, his escalating medical situations, our family, and my work schedule could bear. And Peter understood that very well. So he moved from being the team statistician, to becoming the teams' chief fan. For all the years that followed, he was present at just about every Southwood game he could attend. And he became the best fan Southwood ever had!

Algebra Problems

In the second semester of his eighth-grade year, the guidance department encouraged students and parents to start thinking about going to high school, and what kind of track—college, business, vocational—to choose. With Peter, we'd been so busy just trying to survive and juggle the other balls in our lives that we hadn't really given it much thought. So we decided to sit down with Peter and do some career planning.

Prior to 1987, he'd always said he wanted to be a sports announcer. But now, without being able to talk, I really didn't know what he'd say. So we carefully began the discussion.

"What do you think you want to do in life, Peter?" A very long pause. Finally he spoke.

"I think I'd like to be an assistant coach, or a statistician, or something like that."

I had a dual reaction. My head said, "That's not realistic," but my heart said, "Poor kid—sports are the love of his life, and I don't see how he's ever going to do the kinds of things that he'd otherwise love and be great at."

Trying my best to camouflage some tears, I just said something like, "That sounds good, Pete. You'd probably be really good at something like that."

So we signed him up for an academic track as at least some place to start. As he started his freshman year, he was doing pretty well overall, but algebra was presenting some challenges.

When Roger had been a freshman, I'd help him some, but once would do it. With Peter, it was a different story. I'd help him once, think he had it, and the next night we were right back where we started. At times, I'd get pretty frustrated with him. Then I'd feel guilty because Peter wasn't the type to give a lackadaisical effort. Finally, it hit me. I was the one who wasn't getting the fact that Peter wasn't getting it when it came to algebra. At some point, we dropped the course because there was no way he was going to pass it. We decided to talk to Dr. Turner about it at our next visit.

Dr. Turner set him up with a neuropsychologist in their practice who did psychological testing, and he gave Peter an IQ test. When he explained the results to Peter, he was very professional about it, but Sandra and I were pretty disappointed. As a little kid, all indications were that he was pretty bright. But the test results showed that his

IQ had dropped considerably. Apparently countless surgeries and the incidents of having to be resuscitated, etc., had taken their toll.

For any loss that he'd experienced, however, Peter camouflaged it well. My experience at White's was that kids who were personable tended to come across as brighter than they really were, and Peter was certainly personable. He still did pretty well in his general classes, but struggled considerably with subjects like math, that relied more on native, rather than learned intelligence. In his sophomore year, he took pre-algebra, and really didn't do much better than he had the year before. At the end of the year, his teacher, Mr. Bosler, gave him a D-, which had to be an outright gift, and one for which I have always been grateful.

In years to come, Peter did pretty well in some classes, and actually became a fairly good writer. But keeping his checkbook was another story. Sandra finally concluded that it would be easier to do it herself. That continued to be a pattern, where he performed pretty well in some areas, but could be kind of dense in others.

***

From about the time Peter was in junior high, he stopped growing. As a condition of having been born with spina bifida, his back, which was really pretty messed up, just never got to a normal length. And he'd never used his legs at all since going into the wheelchair, so without normal activity and exercise, those never reached full length either. By virtue of his receiving all of his nutrition, which had been precisely calculated by Dr. Maisel, through his J-tube and feeding pump, he never had the option of "overeating," so he never really gained any more weight.

Had Peter been born normal, I'm guessing he'd have been as big or bigger than Roger, who's a little over six feet and normal build. But he pretty much stabilized at about five feet one and 135 pounds. In many respects that was probably a good thing. We had to do a lot of lifting with Peter, and if he'd have been six feet six and 250 pounds, it could have been a real challenge.

Colts Connections

From 1989 to 1993, Roger attended Anderson University, where he studied sports medicine, with the goal of becoming an athletic trainer in the NFL or for an NCAA team. He did well in his studies, and in his sophomore year, had an opportunity to work training camp as a trainer intern for the Indianapolis Colts, who did their training camp there at Anderson University.

At the time he applied for the internship, Peter was in the hospital, and I prepped Roger for his interview before he ran over to the Colts' complex, while Sandra and I were staying at the Ronald McDonald House. He also got a reference from Dr. Turner, who filled in for Dr. Feuer occasionally on the sidelines as the Colts' neurosurgical consultant. Soon, he was notified that he got the job.

Roger wound up working two training camps, in '91 and '92, plus occasional games during the season, and it was a huge thrill for all of us. We'd try to go down and watch practice as often as we could break away from work. It was cool seeing our son out on the field, doing his duties and interacting with the players. Roger wound up doing various treatments fairly regularly for running back Eric Dickerson, who later was inducted into the Pro Football Hall of Fame. It was also fun seeing famous players, coaches, TV sports personalities, celebrities, stretch limos, and all the excitement that went with a pro sports team. During those years, we saw Roger on TV numerous times, sometimes right in the thick of things.

Our whole family had a blast anytime we'd go to training camp, and although some of the players would try to avoid signing autographs, most were very gracious when they saw Peter. The experience was a thrill for the whole family. We were agreed—it was pretty cool having a son, or big brother, "in the NFL!"

Roger did well in his time with the Colts and had some great opportunities to pursue his dream of being a big-time trainer. But through his internships, he'd also seen the "other side" of professional sports—the eighteen-hour days, intense pressure, time away from family, and some aspects of the lifestyle—and decided that it wasn't for him. Ultimately he became an athletic director, and then a high school guidance counselor.

We were proud of him while he was "in the NFL," and had a lot of fun with it. We're still proud of him.

Boone's Farm

I'd grown up on a farm, and for most of my adult life I'd had the dream of having a small farm of our own, where we could just "play farmer" and have our kids experience some of the special experiences and work ethic that growing up on a farm entails. Finally, in 1988, I got my chance.

A twenty-seven-acre farm just north of White's came up for sale, with someone else wanting to buy the house. Farmland was still cheap, as the farm economy hadn't yet recovered from the farm recession earlier that decade. So we borrowed the money and took the plunge! With a demanding job and Peter's situation, I'm sure some people must have thought we were nuts. But it wound up being one of the best decisions of our lives.

It wasn't any great farm by most standards—only about sixteen of the twenty-seven acres were tillable, and it was very average-quality land. But it had "character"—gently rolling, some woods, and an old bank barn with a limestone foundation. And we loved it! The kids could have a place of our own for their 4-H animals, I could reclaim some permanent pasture and raise a few cattle, and Sandra could have a horse.

I bought an old John Deere tractor and a Bush Hog rotary mower to mow pasture and side ditches. A neighbor, Dave Ridenour, farmed the tillable part for us, which allowed us to "just have fun." After working all day in a stress-filled job in social work, a change into old clothes and a farmer's cap, a two-minute drive, and I was on my tractor, or tending animals, or driving a steel post, in a totally different world. It was good for my soul. Years later, Sandra and I built a new home on the back corner of the place.

Roger, Peter, and Philip were able to participate in farm life to varying degrees. Peter was able to participate the least, and never really became a "farm kid." But he enjoyed seeing his 4-H pigs and watching our cattle when he could.

But for Sandra and me, it was a welcome and very healthy balance to the rest of the craziness in our lives. One of the great things about farming is that it's so tangible—for better or worse, at the end of the day, you pretty much know what you have or haven't accomplished. In my world with troubled kids and Peter, where tangibles were often hard to find, the farm was my salvation.

The Amazing Impact of a Thoughtful Gesture

When Peter was a little kid, picking him up or lifting him was no big deal. But as he got older and bigger, it became more challenging. He'd shared the lower part of a bunk bed with Philip, and Peter's heavier weight and whacking our heads on the bottom of Philip's bunk were getting old.

One day we got a phone call from Janet Aswegan, one of our friends and former coworkers at White's. She'd been by the local hospital, and they were trying to get rid of some of their old hospital beds for only $15 each, and wanted to know if we'd be interested in one. It sounded like a deal, so we quickly said yes. Someone actually brought it to our house for us. It was a real antique, but it worked well.

Once there, it seemed like it weighed half a ton and was an absolute bear to get through the house and into Peter's room. Janet's husband, Jim, who was an ag mechanic at the time, fabricated a heavy-duty lift bar that attached to the head of the bed, so Peter could help lift himself when getting in and out. Then Jim painted the whole thing gold, and lettered "Pulling for Purdue" on the side.

Over the years, Sandra and I both developed some back problems from lifting Peter. She actually had two back surgeries. Both of our backs would have been so much worse, however, without that phone call. That old bed wound up in three different houses over three decades, and faithfully performed its simple duties every single morning and night. It not only saved our backs, and the backs of our respite care providers, but brought Peter up to a much more workable level that made it easier for all of us to care for him and interact with him.

Fifteen dollars for thirty years of back-saving benefits was one of the best investments of my life. But Janet's taking five minutes to call us because she was looking for ways to help us out was one of the best investments of time and caring I've ever experienced.

CHAPTER 13
BLESSED ARE THOSE WHO PROVIDE RESPITE

Being a caregiver for a family member with chronic medical conditions takes a tremendous toll on both caregivers and marriages. But one huge thing God did to help Sandra and me in that regard was to bring some truly amazing people into our lives to come alongside of us and provide respite—give us a break—that was an absolute lifesaver for us. Sometimes for an evening, sometimes for a weekend, occasionally for a week, these individuals would take a turn at taking care of Peter for us.

Part of that included "getting hands-on (or in)" in some of the messier aspects of caring for someone with serious disabilities. But they reached right in anyway, which allowed us to have something of a life besides just being Peter's parents and caregivers. And it brought some key people into Peter's life, who made indelible impressions on both him and us. They enriched his life, and he, theirs. And they all brought something unique to the table. Peter, Sandra, and I were the beneficiaries, and we literally couldn't have survived without them.

Below are the primary people who stepped up to fill those roles.

Beverly

From day one, Sandra's mom was there for us. Actually, all of her family—her dad, sisters, brother, and their spouses and children—were great when it came to supporting us with Peter. But Beverly particularly was an ever-present help in countless ways for decades. One of those key ways was caring for Peter while we were gone, and staying with all three boys.

Beverly was probably one of the most giving, sweet-spirited people I've ever known—not your stereotypical mother-in-law—and a better Christian than I've ever thought about being. And she was fun-loving, a joy to have around, never obtrusive about being there for us, and just glad to help in whatever way she could.

And she loved Peter unconditionally. She loved talking with him, caring for him, helping him with homework, altering clothes to fit his misshapen little body, helping him endlessly sort his football card collection, buying him his first computer, staying with him at the hospital, and a thousand other things. From the day he was born, Peter was her special project.

***

Sandra's parents lived about fifteen miles away, and one evening during Peter's lengthy hospitalization in 1984, she came up to check how the rest of us were doing while Sandra stayed at Methodist Hospital with Peter. She said something about she'd have to get up soon and help out with a little housecleaning. I was a little taken aback.

"I've been trying to keep everything clean, and I thought I was doing pretty well," I said, a little defensively. She just smiled sweetly.

"You have; you've done a great job," she assured me. "But it just needs a little bit of a woman's touch."

***

Years later, she was staying with Peter while Sandra and I got away for the weekend. Roger and Philip were already gone by then, so in typical Grandma fashion, she wanted Peter to have a good time, so she had three of his younger cousins—Zach, Aaron, and Chris—come up and stay with her and Peter. And have a good time they did!

Peter was already in bed for the night and hooked up to the ventilator and his other equipment. The four of them were playing video games in his room and generally fooling around, trying to be quiet, but laughing and having a great time into the wee hours of the morning. Grandma had told them a couple of times to go to bed, but they were having too good a time, and she finally fell asleep.

Anyway, in a somewhat perverse, but nevertheless "boys-will-be-boys" manner, the three cousins were entertaining themselves by having a contest to see who could pass the most obnoxious-smelling gas. The lead in this dubious competition changed hands a number of times, while Peter was trapped in bed, forced to inhale the methane-rich results of these goings-on.

Then Peter took control. By that time he had a colostomy, and the smell from it was truly otherworldly. Seeing an opportunity to turn his medical condition to his advantage, he pretended to accidently drop a pencil from his bedside stand onto the floor, and it rolled under the bed. While Zach was retrieving it, Peter released some gas from the ostomy bag. It took a few seconds before the smell reached the boys, who weren't accustomed to it. Zach, who was still under the bed and closest, started yelling and thought he was going to throw up. Then all three ran out of the room, gagging and coughing, while Peter nearly laughed himself into a coma.

"He totally blew us away," recalled Zach. "That was the end of that contest."

And another example of Beverly going above and beyond to make life fun for Peter. And making great memories for four cousins in ways she could have never imagined.

***

As the years passed, Sandra recognized that Beverly wasn't as sharp on Peter's care as she'd been in years past, and gradually moved away from having her provide respite for us. But Beverly still was a faithful friend and grandma to Peter.

Then at about age seventy-two, Beverly was diagnosed with Alzheimer's. Her descent into this awful disease was heartbreaking. After several years at home, Sandra's dad was no longer able to care for her, and she was placed in a nursing home in LaFontaine, just a few miles from us.

With the shoe now on the other foot, Peter became one of her most faithful visitors. After work he'd slip down there and talk with her, and, later, when she could no longer carry on a conversation, would just hang out with her.

After twelve years, Beverly finally died in September 2013. Along with the rest of his cousins, Peter was an honorary pallbearer.

Beverly was the best.

Sandy

"I just felt that God was laying on my heart that I needed to be my brother's keeper, and be a good neighbor," recalled Sandy Davis. "And you guys lived next to us, so you were our neighbors."

Rich and Sandy lived next to us on the White's campus for a dozen years or so while both our kids and theirs were growing up. Although Rich was the executive director of White's Residential and Family Services, which made him our boss, and Sandy his secretary, when we weren't at work, they were "just neighbors." Our kids—including Peter in his scooter—and theirs used to play baseball in the yard that lay between their house and ours. And what neighbors they turned out to be!

I first remember Sandy getting involved in Peter's care when she volunteered to help pull bathroom duty for Peter at Southwood Elementary. Then, later on, she started coming to our house twice a week, for roughly an hour or so each night, to do respite for us. Then she started spelling Sandra and me for breaks from the hospital during long stays. She was staying with Peter at Methodist Hospital when he suddenly needed emergency surgery for a gangrene-infested bowel during the middle of the night. When Peter was in the hospital, and both Sandra and I had to be there, Sandy and Rich would have Roger and Philip stay at their home, where our boys became "adjunct family." She also stepped up big time later during two of the roughest stretches in our lives. But more about that later. Over time, they developed a close relationship.

"Peter was one of my best friends," recalled Sandy. "Whether I was having a good day or a bad day, I knew I could tell him whatever was going on in my life, and it wouldn't go any further. And he would do the same with me."

And then, in '97, Rich and Sandy felt the call to go to Kenya as missionaries. They were there for seven years. When they got back, they accepted pastoral positions in our church and purchased a home about four miles away. And Sandy started doing respite again, picking up right where she left off.

Most of the time when Sandy was doing all of these things, it wasn't like she had a lot of extra time. Between being the executive director's secretary, very active in our church, a busy social schedule, and having three children and later grandchildren with activities of their own, she still always managed to find time to say, "How can I help?"

"I just made it a priority and worked it into my schedule," she said.

Were Rich and Sandy good neighbors? God couldn't have provided better. But besides a treasury of good, difficult, and funny memories, Sandy said her decades of caring for Peter did include some nifty fringe benefits.

"When I took care of Pete, he loved to watch *The Andy Griffith Show*," she said. "I think I've seen just about every episode."

Jerry

When Rich and Sandy made the decision to go to Kenya as missionaries, we were in a quandary. Beverly was no longer able to do respite. And not just anybody could either want to take the responsibility of taking care of Peter's considerable needs, or be the kind of caring person we'd feel comfortable with trusting with Peter. We'd come to the place where we recognized that for us, respite was a need, not just a want. But where would we ever find such an individual?

As we prayed for an answer, it finally hit us. Sandy Carter, Peter's second-grade teacher, would be great for that role, if she was willing.

After struggling with some health issues, including a liver transplant at the Mayo Clinic, Sandy had been forced into an early retirement from teaching, but seemed to have recovered nicely. So we called her up and asked if we could come to her home and talk to her about something.

As we talked with Sandy about the possibility, she was looking pretty uncomfortable about the idea. Finally she said that she'd love to, but that with her liver transplant, she'd been told not to be around any bodily fluids, etc.

Immediately, both Sandra and I were dejected, thinking, *Nuts, now where do we go?*

Then her husband, Jerry, said quietly, "I'll do that."

What? We knew Jerry somewhat, but the thought that'd he volunteer for a mission like this never remotely crossed our minds. As we talked with him, it soon became clear that he was both serious, and realized the scope of what he'd offered to do.

Soon, we gave Jerry some orientation, and he was off and running. He never stayed overnight with Peter, but for about seven years, he'd come faithfully, twice a week, and spend an hour or more, helping with Peter's nighttime routine, which provided us a much-needed break. He became Peter's friend.

And as we got to know him better, Jerry became our friend too. When we were ready to move into our new house, he wallpapered the whole house for us!

Jerry had some health issues of his own. He was seriously diabetic, and also suffered from bouts of depression. He had sold the Chrysler dealership he'd owned in Wabash in order to take care of his wife as she went through her liver transplant. He keenly felt the loss of his life's work.

One time when we were telling him how much we appreciated him and what he was doing for all of us, he said, "When a man can no longer earn a living, it does a number on him. This is giving me an opportunity to feel useful again."

Eventually Jerry stepped down from doing respite for Peter. But for those years, he helped us fill a vital need. Apparently caring for Peter filled a need for him too.

Tim

I had worked with Tim and Deb Main when they were child-care workers at White's, and then later Tim became the head groundskeeper there. When Rich and Sandy Davis were preparing to go to Africa, Sandy approached Tim and asked if he could be praying about someone to take her place providing respite care for Peter while they were gone.

"She never asked me, 'Will you do it?' She just asked me to pray about it," recalled Tim. "But then I got to thinking, *There's no reason I can't do that; I can learn whatever I need to learn.*"

So he came over with Sandy a couple of times before they left to shadow her. But by then, Jerry Carter was helping us, so we just used Tim initially for those times when Jerry couldn't be there. Then when Jerry stepped down, Tim began coming twice a week like Sandy had.

I always talked a lot of sports with Peter, but Tim has a sweatshirt that says "Unathletic Department," so sports wasn't a big part of their time together. Instead, they'd talk about mutual interests that I couldn't relate to, but which were important to Peter. Things like contemporary Christian music (I'm a traditional guy), computers, concerts, and later, a disability camp that they attended together, with Tim as Peter's caregiver. They became very good friends. If it would normally take about an hour to get Peter ready for bed, often Tim would be there two hours—one hour of respite, and another hour of "whatever."

"We'd also share what was going on in each of our lives—school, work, family, his cousins, and more," said Tim. "And on those occasions where I'd cover an overnight with Peter, he'd really get excited about being able to do some kind of special activity together."

Tim lost track of how many Christian concerts they went to, but it was a lot, with Michael W. Smith leading the pack. Most of the time it was just Peter and Tim, but occasionally Deb would go with them.

One of the things that struck Tim about Peter was the fact that he never complained about the medical aspects of his life.

"Oh, he'd complain about the normal stuff that everybody complains about, but I never once heard him complain about his physical problems," he said. "But I knew what it took for him to just get through each day, and if there was ever anybody who had things to complain about, it was him. For me, it was a good reminder to 'Get a grip, deal with it, and move on, Tim. You have nothing to complain about.'"

Shelly

Phil's wife, Shelly, came into our lives when she married Phil in 2004, and she is a nurse practitioner. The first time the possibility of her taking care of Peter for us came up in 2009 when Sandra and I were contemplating going to Maui to celebrate our fortieth anniversary. She offered to stay at our house and do a good bit of his care for a little over a week.

My first thought was, *Peter surely wouldn't be interested in that. If I were in his shoes, I sure wouldn't want my sisters-in-law giving me baths, and everything else that would go along with taking care of me. I'm also guessing they wouldn't exactly be jumping at that opportunity either!*

But despite being my son, Peter was very much his own person, and didn't have a problem with it. However I still couldn't imagine it. Yes, she was a medical professional, and, yes, Peter had been cared for by hundreds of nurses and other respite care providers, all of whom had seen him in all kinds of circumstances. But his sister-in-law?

But Sandra and I really wanted to go to Maui, so at some point we figured that if the two of them were willing, we guessed we'd try it. And it worked out great! It turned out to be a wonderful break for us, and I think for Peter, it was probably a welcome break from us. Shelly seemed to really have enjoyed it too.

"From a clinical standpoint, taking care of Peter was super

interesting," she said. "He had so many conditions wrong with him that I'd never seen before and probably will never see again, that it was really a learning experience, a fascinating case study. Also, I didn't have to worry about running into something I couldn't handle, because Peter knew his own care so well. If I started to feel stumped, I'd just say, 'Pete, what do I do now,' and he always knew."

And so Shelly moved into a position of being our backup, go-to respite care provider for certain occasions where Tim or Sandy couldn't cover. And rather than seeing it as a chore or obligation, she actually looked forward to it, even with a ventilator that would sometimes keep beeping in the middle of the night, or waking her up at 2:00 a.m. to find that his ostomy bag had sprung a leak, and there was a huge mess in the bed and on the floor.

"I loved being able to take care of Peter because he was very special to me, and it was a very special time for me to really hear what he was thinking and what was going on in his world," she said. "Joni [Joni Eareckson Tada, well-known disability advocate] talks about co-laboring with those who have physical or mental challenges, to help them be all that they can be, and that was what I felt like I was doing when I took care of Peter. Peter could 'go' pretty much into the normal world, but he needed help to get there. I loved being in a position to help him do that."

Occasionally Shelly and Peter's conversations would go to a deeper level.

"My best memory of taking care of Peter came one time when I was taking care of him when we were at the lake," she recalled. "We were just talking about anything and everything, and somehow our conversation moved to talking about when we get to heaven. I wound up telling him, 'Pete, if you beat me there, I expect to see you standing there at the Pearly Gates. I can't wait to see you standing. And I expect you to pick me up and twirl me around when I get there.'"

"I will, Shelly," he said. "You can count on it."

CHAPTER 14
DODGING BULLETS

Over the course of Peter's life, we lost track of the number of close calls we'd had, when we really didn't think he was going to make it. There were a number of times in the hospital when it seemed the end was near. There was a time at Children's Hospital in Cincinnati where he received CPR for forty-five minutes.

Then there was a time at Purdue. We were tailgating with friends from church on a beautiful fall day before the start of the 2004 Ohio State-Purdue game, and everyone was having a great time. Peter somehow got choked, went unconscious, then unresponsive, and attempts to revive him weren't working. I thought it was over. Then a doctor tailgating nearby suddenly came to his rescue, and cleared his airway; then an ambulance whisked him away to St. Elizabeth's Hospital across the river in Lafayette. He wound up watching the second half of the game from his hospital room, which Purdue won in a thriller, 24–17.

But of all Peter's near-death experiences, the one that sticks out most in my mind occurred on May 30, 1991.

Thank God for Dirty Pistons

Peter had been in Methodist Hospital's ICU for a couple weeks with some very serious infectious issues, and things hadn't been going well. I was home at work, and that day while I was attending morning chapel at White's, I got a call from Sandra. Peter had stopped breathing, and they'd had to resuscitate him, and things weren't looking good. She told me to get down there as soon as I could.

I shattered speed limits all the way there. By the time I arrived, he was doing slightly better, but his situation was still dire. Our associate pastor, Doug DaFoe, who, despite being a Michigan Wolverine fan, had a great relationship with Peter, came down to be there with all of us as soon as he got word.

At some point, things started to head south. The doctors asked us to step out for a few minutes, and then had us come back in, essentially to tell him good-bye. I remember they had dimmed the lights in the multi-bed ICU, apparently wanting to give us as much privacy as possible. Dr. Williams, the ICU chief, was very somber. The ICU was almost silent, except for the gentle whirr and occasional beeps of the monitors and ventilators. Peter's color was getting pretty gray. A social worker came up and put her hand on his arm, and tearfully said, "We love you, Peter."

Our son was dying. I was standing there by his bedside while Sandra and Doug were trying to get themselves composed behind me. This was the moment I had feared for nearly sixteen years would be coming someday. Yet now it was here, yet I felt wholly unprepared.

At that instant, I wanted to tell Peter that I loved him, but my instincts said *not* to. My very strong gut feel was that Peter knew me well enough that if I told him that I loved him at that critical moment, he'd know immediately that "it's over," and he would slip away, and I didn't want to let him go. But if not that, what do I say? I breathed a very quick, desperate, silent prayer.

Suddenly an answer came to me. "Why don't you do what you always do—talk with him about sports?" So I did. Putting my hand on his arm and struggling for words, I gamely said, "What time's the game tonight, Pete?" referring to the NBA playoff game between the Chicago Bulls and the Detroit Pistons. He smiled weakly, and told me he thought it started at eight. Then our conversation took a totally unexpected turn.

"You know what, Dad? Those Pistons are *dirty!*"

"What?"

"Yeah, they really are!" he continued, very agitated. "Did you see what they've been doing to Michael Jordan? They're trying to beat him up every chance they get, just trying to intimidate him and mess up his game! They've even been knocking him out of bounds when they foul him on some of his jump shots!"

I was in total disbelief. Here's our son, who by all reasonable measures is dying. And he's going off about the game tactics of the "Bad Boys" Detroit Pistons?

He was on a real rant. He was *mad* because some Detroit player, Dennis Rodman, I think, was abusing his favorite player. The refs weren't doing enough about it, and he was *sick* of it!

This was a truly surreal moment.

But then slowly, imperceptibly at first, his color began to come back, ever so slightly. He continued his rant. His color continued to improve. As he further vented his frustrations, the crisis passed, and he stabilized. He had a couple of more crisis episodes that day, but not nearly as serious as this one.

I'm not a medical person, but to this day I truly believe that had I not inadvertently pushed that hot button for him, he would have drifted off into eternity. I think God answered my desperate prayer in an unmistakable way, and gave me just the right—albeit unorthodox—words to say in that situation. I think his passion for sports triggered a shot of adrenalin that literally saved his life.

Course Corrections

Experiences like the one just described and other similar ones wound up changing my thinking on some things. At some point, Peter had dodged so many bullets that I pretty much came to believe that he was "bulletproof." Peter was an incredibly tough kid, who survived things that would have done in many strong adults.

Sandra would often say, "God's not done with him yet. He still has a plan for Peter," which I believed completely. But I also think that

Peter, despite all his challenges, had figured out so many ways to enjoy his life, through the things most of us take for granted, that he just wasn't ready to go yet. He was having too much fun to die!

I also decided during this time that I was done riding the roller coaster of emotions that were part of the baggage of Peter's life. When he was in serious trouble, I was totally down in the dumps, and basically prepared myself for the worst. Then when he'd recover, the joy was exhilarating! We'd assume that we had the worst behind us, and could move on to better things. Then some new crisis would come up, hijack my emotions, and I'd go through it all over again. At this point I reached the conclusion that I couldn't do this anymore. I *wouldn't* do this anymore.

So I basically put my emotions on autopilot, drew some firm upper and lower limits of how high or low I'd allow them to go. On those times when he was at his worst, I would no longer allow myself to assume that this was "the big one." And when he recovered, I no longer ventured into "whew-I'm-glad-we've-left-that-behind" territory.

The truth was that Peter was a mix of incredible medical complexities, and anything could happen to him at any moment. I had to accept that. But he had also demonstrated an incredible mental toughness, greater than that of most any linebacker he'd ever watched on TV. For the sake of my own emotional health, as well as my role as a husband, dad, and for the rest of the important pieces of our lives, I needed to get off the roller coaster. I never got back on.

CHAPTER 15
1993: DOUBLE TROUBLE

As our family turned the calendar to 1993, it was a mixed bag. Since 1991, Peter had been fighting pressure sores, caused by the deformity in his back and aggravated by poor circulation. He'd had some surgeries for skin grafting but was going to need more. We were doing our best to put it off until summer, so he wouldn't have to miss any more school than necessary.

But on a brighter note, Roger would be graduating from Anderson University in May, and, the week after, he was getting married. While studying sports medicine, he'd met Tonya, a pretty softball player from Kentucky, in AU's training room. He'd treated her for an elbow injury, asked her out to a Cincinnati Reds game, and the rest was history!

Our whole family was excited! For Sandra particularly, it meant finally having a girl in the family, after patiently putting up with a house full of males her entire adult life. And Peter gave his wholehearted approval. Besides her other prerequisite qualifications, she could hold her own talking sports with him!

Discovery

Sometime in late February, Sandra noticed a lump in one of her breasts. We made an appointment to get it checked out right away, but otherwise didn't think all that much about it. A number of women in our circle of friends and family had had fibroid cysts recently, and the thought that she might actually have "the big C," with everything else going on, didn't seem a likely possibility.

But that's exactly what it turned out to be. After waiting what seemed like forever to get test results back, it did show that it was a malignant tumor. Soon she had surgery, with tissue and lymph nodes analyzed further. After what seemed like another eternity, those results showed that the cancer was stage II/III, her lymph nodes showed cancer cells, and the tumor was described as "aggressive and invasive."

Our surgeon referred us to an oncologist, Dr. Steven Meyer, in Fort Wayne. When we met Dr. Meyer, we liked him instantly, and he seemed to relate well to Sandra. We figured he'd get her started on chemotherapy and radiation, and she was ready to get on with it.

Instead, he told us that her type of cancer was a serious threat to her life, and that he was recommending a bone marrow transplant at Duke University Med Center in North Carolina, one of the premier cancer treatment facilities in the world. Both of us could have passed out! We felt as if someone had just dropped a bomb on us, which he in fact had.

He told us that the treatment was extremely severe, but that he thought it was her best option for recovery. He then asked her if she wanted to do it. I was still feeling as if I'd just had my bell rung, but without hesitation, she responded, "Yes, I want to live."

Soon after, Dr. Meyer started her on a regular chemo protocol, which would precede the big-gun treatment she would receive in North Carolina. Then in early April, the two of us made our first trip to Duke, where she had to have an interview and be screened further before being accepted into the bone marrow transplant program. While we were there on serious business, we immediately fell in love with the area and the Duke campus. North Carolina was beautiful that time of the year, and the campus was too. Sandra was accepted into the program, and was scheduled to start her treatment in June.

Throughout all of this, Peter really seemed to be the most at peace of any of us. One day he told Sandra, "Mom, if I can get through all I've been through, you can handle this." And from Peter's frame of reference, that was pretty much all there was to it. When he ran into any of his many difficulties, he just dealt with it, did what had to be done, lots of people prayed for him, God was in charge, and eventually he always came out the other end of the tunnel. That's just the way it worked.

For both Sandra and I, it was really very reassuring, and the jolt of a different perspective that we needed badly. Peter may have only been seventeen, but he'd clearly "paid his dues." He'd earned the right to speak with authority in these matters.

But First ...

But before that, we had some other items to take care of. Roger graduated on Sunday, May 9, and the wedding was scheduled in Anderson on May 15, the following Saturday. By that time, Sandra was really beginning to feel the effects of the chemo. But there were a succession of bridal showers before the wedding, and her excitement had gotten her through those pretty well.

While on chemo, a patient cycles through periods of feeling pretty good with decent immunity, and feeling horrible, with poor immunity. May 15 looked to be one of the latter times. After the rehearsal dinner on the night before, Rich and Sandy Davis told us to stay in a hotel in Anderson, and said they'd stay with and take care of Philip and Peter, who Roger had asked to be his best man. Peter was honored to be asked, and was pretty pumped about his "official duties."

As Rich and Sandy got Peter into his tuxedo Saturday morning, his dress shoes kept slipping off the floor of his scooter, so in desperation, Rich cut the black welcome mat to our house in two, turned it upside down, and it worked perfectly!

By that time, Sandra had lost a good part of her hair, and the rehearsal dinner and wedding were the first times she'd worn her wig. But she looked great in her pink dress and "new hair," and no one ever knew. And the excitement of the day carried her.

We'd had some concerns about Peter being the best man. How would he get up on the platform? What if he had to suction during the vows? But things went great. Rich and Sandy had brought his portable ramp, and suctioning didn't turn out to be an issue. He actually looked pretty cool as he cocked his elbow to accompany the maid of honor down the aisle, smiling all the way.

The night before, Sandy had helped him write his toast to the bride and groom, which one of the other groomsmen read for him. Most of it was Peter's doing, and it was really pretty good—appropriate, funny, witty. The main thing I remember was that he thanked the bride and groom for "scheduling their wedding on a day when the Chicago Bulls didn't have a playoff game."

Going to Duke

Wedding over, it was time to refocus on fighting cancer. Sandra had to go down to Duke for a couple of weeks before the actual bone marrow transplant to do some preliminary treatments and such. Her sister Brenda and friend Patty DeVore took her down, and the two of them helped keep her spirits up. She left on the morning of June 13, a Sunday on my duty weekend.

But at home I was struggling. I'd never felt more helpless or alone in my life. Not only did I have Peter with all his challenges, but my wife was in North Carolina being treated for a serious case of cancer. I prayed a lot more than usual during those days. But of all my pleas to God, the dominant theme was, "Please, God, don't let anything happen to her. If it does, Peter and I will both go down the tubes."

The next day, I was getting some things in place before I went down to be with her during her actual transplant and a few weeks to follow. I went north of Wabash to buy a pickup load of hay for Sandra's horse. As I knocked on the farmhouse door, the wife was on the phone, and motioned me to step in. In the course of doing so, I must have said something, and the person on the other end recognized my voice.

It was Rosie Custer, a dear lady from our church. She told the lady about our circumstances and how they'd been praying for us. I was overwhelmed. It seemed to me that it was a message from God to me through Rosie—something like, "It's okay. I know exactly where you are and how to get in touch with you. There are many people praying for you, and I'm listening. I'm in this with you."

I kept my composure until I got the hay loaded, then I cried all the way home.

***

Another tangible demonstration of God's presence with us occurred before Sandra went down to Duke. One of our big concerns before Sandra left was paying for the treatment. Duke's approach to doing bone marrow transplants of this type was to have a few days of super-high-dose chemo in the hospital, followed four weeks or so of follow-up treatment in a clinic, while the patients lived in a hotel next to the clinic. I was to be her caregiver during that time.

All this was cutting edge, enough so that our health insurance company—one of the biggest—was balking at paying, describing it as experimental, and was dragging its heels. Duke's position was that the bone marrow transplant procedure had proved itself as a cost-effective alternative to more conventional bone marrow transplant procedures at the time, which required several weeks of isolation in an ICU. Part of Duke's approach was to make transplants more affordable for more women.

As time got closer, I discussed this with our attorney, Mark Guenin, who attended our church. Mark may have been a small-town attorney, but he was not one to back down from this big-city Goliath. He took our case, and after doing his due diligence, threatened the insurance company with seeking a summary judgment against them if they didn't step up to assume their responsibilities, and quick! And a few days before Sandra left for North Carolina, Mark called us, saying the company had agreed to pay. Needless to say, it was a huge relief to us.

I'd arranged to borrow the money, but it would have taken us the rest of our lives to dig our way out of that financial hole.

"It was one of the coolest things I've ever been involved with," Mark said afterward. "Our fax machine churned out page after page of documentation from Duke that demonstrated that the treatment was past the 'experimental' stage. It was really pretty exciting."

He never charged us a dime for his services.

**

After two weeks, White's worked with me to string all my vacation and sick days together to carve out a leave of absence for myself, and I went down to be with Sandra for the duration of her time there. During the time I was to be gone, Sandra's mom and Sandy Davis would be tag-teaming the lion's share of Peter's considerable care, with help from several others, which was a godsend.

When I got down to Duke, she was feeling reasonably good, and we had a few days of preliminary treatments before she started the actual bone marrow transplant. We used that extra time as an opportunity to tour the area and the campus.

At Duke's basketball arena, Cameron Indoor Stadium, they had summer basketball camps going on, and one day she got to meet Duke's coach, Mike Krzyzewski. She'd seen him on TV and had remarked that compared to many of the other volatile college coaches, he "seemed like such a nice man," and he became one of her heroes. From that point on, the rest of us teased her mercilessly about "the nice man," and she'd finally got to meet him.

I'd call home daily, to update the people there, and vice versa. Every day when I'd call, Peter would have some bit of sports news for me. He'd write it out, and then have Sandra's mom read it to me. I also told him about Mom meeting "the nice man," which he thought was a hoot. With mostly women around the house now, I think he missed having someone to talk sports with.

**

One of my initial concerns when I first got down to Duke was that Peter's back was in serious need of more surgeries for pressure sores. But I was already down in Durham, North Carolina, with Sandra, and had no idea how we'd handle things if Peter had to go in for more surgery in Indianapolis.

One day when I called home, Sandra's parents had taken him down to Indianapolis for an appointment with Dr. Turner. Although Dr. Turner was a neurosurgeon, he knew Peter's overall situation very well. As Sandra's mom told him what else was going on in our family, he said simply, "You tell him to take care of Sandra first. Peter will be okay until Duke gets her fixed up."

Hearing that was a bigger relief than I have words to describe. And as usual, Dr. Turner was right.

The Transplant

As we learned prior to the actual transplant, Sandra's bone marrow wasn't the reason she needed a bone marrow transplant. Instead, the essence of the treatment was that she would be receiving super-high-dose chemo therapy, far beyond normal chemo regimens, to kill the cancer. In the process, the treatment was harsh enough that a patient's bone marrow would essentially be killed off, requiring new bone marrow to be transplanted.

Sandra's was what was known as an autologous transplant, where the patient becomes his or her own donor. Prior to the actual transplant, doctors had extracted a couple quarts of bone marrow from her hip bones, which they would save until afterward to reinject and jump-start the growth of new bone marrow. We'd been told ahead of time that the transplant process would largely do everything but kill the patient in order to kill the cancer, and that it would probably be the most difficult experience of her life. It was at least that.

The transplant procedure started off at Duke North Hospital with about four or five days of the high-dose chemo, during which Sandra would mostly be asleep and remember little of it. Then she would be discharged from the hospital to the Hampton Inn, a few miles north of the hospital, next to the Bone Marrow Transplant clinic, and I would be her caregiver. That was the hard part.

By this time, the patients were very sick. As we made our daily treks next door to the clinic, we'd pass many other women, wearing caps or other coverings for their bald heads and carrying plastic pans to throw up in, which happened often and without warning. At first it was pretty gross, but soon it became "just normal." There were also other troublesome side effects.

I felt so badly for those women, including Sandra, and I also developed a very strong admiration for them and their courage. Guys pride themselves on being strong and macho. I'm not at all sure I could have handled a bone marrow transplant.

Sandra couldn't eat anything except the mildest of bland food or popsicles, and often she'd even throw them up. She was on a ton of meds, many of which she'd throw up too. At one point, she spiked a high temperature and had to go back into the hospital ICU for a few days, toxic from everything. At times her face was swollen almost beyond recognition. I had some questions about whether she was going to survive this. This was the lowest time of her life, both physically and emotionally.

As I did my daily morning devotions from *Our Daily Bread,* I was amazed how many of the messages seemed to speak directly to me. One morning particularly, the scripture reference was from Romans 8:28–39. Verses such as, "And we know that all things work together for good to those who love God, to those who are called to His purpose," and "For I am persuaded that neither death nor life, nor angels or principalities nor powers, nor things present nor things to come, nor height nor depth, nor any other created thing, shall be able to separate us from the love of God which is in Christ Jesus our Lord." I needed some serious love during those days, and God delivered it regularly.

***

But very gradually, things began to improve somewhat, and she was finally released in mid-July after about five weeks of the BMT treatment. When she got home, she still had to go through radiation, and pretty much felt miserable for the rest of the year. She returned to picking up some of Peter's care, and basically spent the rest of the time in bed feeling horrible. There were times I still wasn't sure she was going to make it.

But into early 1994, she started feeling somewhat better, and her hair began to return. She, and we, had survived the bone marrow transplant! And God had been there with us.

White's was also right there with us, through everything. Besides being a supportive, caring employer and environment, they also stuck with us through a period when Peter and Sandra were both running up horrendous hospital bills, raising insurance premiums. There had to be times White's administrators wished we'd just go away. Fortunately for us, they never made us do that.

CHAPTER 16
1994: VALLEYS AND MOUNTAINTOPS

As 1993 rolled swiftly into 1994, our lives were still in a considerable state of crisis. Sandra was still very slowly recovering from the bone marrow transplant. Peter's skin grafting for his back had been put on hold until Sandra could regain some traction. But rather suddenly, the pressure sores on his back had gotten much larger, and we were approaching a state of emergency.

His plastic surgeon, Dr. Sadove, scheduled the surgery as an emergency in very early December. The surgery was to do a "skin flap," whereby healthy skin was rotated from one part of Peter's side or back to another. The surgery took six and a half hours, after which Dr. Sadove looked exhausted. And the surgery was not without considerable risk. Rotating skin thusly was never as good as the original skin. If this didn't work, then what? He'd already had enough grafting that Sandra and I were afraid they were going to run out of good skin to graft. And the recuperation would be very lengthy. Peter would be spending the next several weeks or months in the Riley Hospital Burn Unit—not because he had burns, but because his skin grafting procedures were very similar to those who had had serious burn injuries.

Peter wanted to be able to graduate with his class in the worst way, but now this was in doubt. I talked with him about the possibility that he might have to delay graduation a year if things didn't work out, but he would hear none of it.

"No way do I want to do that," he said emphatically. "The kids in my class are my friends, classmates, and teammates. They've been great to me through everything I've been through, and I want to graduate with them. If I had to wait a year, it just wouldn't be the same."

And he was right. As challenging as it might be, Sandra and I wanted as badly as he did to see that happen. We didn't know if we could pull it off but wanted to give it our best shot, and so we got busy trying to figure things out.

It would wind up something over three months that Peter spent in the Burn Unit. But Southwood was great about getting us his assignments. An arrangement was worked out between our school corporation and Indianapolis Public Schools to have an in-hospital teacher work with him to keep him up to speed. For much of the time, Peter had to lie flat on his back on a special mattress, which made reading difficult. So my dad, who was an excellent carpenter, fixed up a device with a piece of Plexiglas that hung flat above Peter's bed so books could be laid flat on it and Peter could read. Someone just had to turn the pages for him. Sandra helped tutor him some, when she was able. Sandy Davis spent quite a few days with Pete, and also helped tutor him.

In ICU, patients have fewer nurses, who spend more time with each individual patient. Peter's primary nurse during this time was an excellent and attractive nurse, an IU grad named Sharon who loved basketball and could talk endlessly with Peter about it. A perfect match! They discussed and argued good-naturedly for most of the time he was there.

Weeks turned into months. At times the doctors would feel like we were making progress. At other times, there was genuine concern that Peter was going to lose the skin flap. But gradually—very gradually—his back started to heal. It continued to get better. But by now we had learned that skin grafts heal extremely slowly, if at all, and that patience was an absolute requirement.

Answer to Prayer Is a "W"

During the winter, I'd try to get my exercise by walking laps in one of White's two gyms. Sometimes I'd go at night and walk with the lights off, just to have some alone time, and sometimes have a prayer time when I got done walking. During the months that Peter was in the Riley Burn Unit, I was really feeling the heaviness of it all. Would he *ever* get out of there? Would he *ever* get skin to successfully grow on his back again? Would he *ever* be able to graduate with his class?

One night after I got done walking, I tried to pray, but just wound up "humming hymns." At first read, that probably sounds pretty stupid, but the truth is that I was feeling so low at that point that I didn't have the mental or spiritual strength to even get the words out. So I'd just hum them. In the Bible it says that God hears and understands the Holy Spirit's groanings, so I figured he could probably understand my humming too. It was basically a way of saying, *"HELP!"* which over the years, I'd found to be one of my most effective prayers. But old hymns such as "Sweet Hour of Prayer," "What a Friend We Have in Jesus," and "I Need Thee Every Hour" comforted me greatly. Even if I didn't have the strength to articulate the words, I still knew them, and they spoke to me.

At some point, my thoughts strayed. Peter had been in the hospital what seemed like an eternity; we had no idea how much longer he'd be there, and I wanted to do something to try to brighten his stay a little. Years ago, Peter's Uncle Mike, an athletic director, had arranged for the Purdue TV crew to tell him "Hi" during a game broadcast. Maybe I could do that again. Then I had this idea. What if I could get Dick Vitale to do that on national TV?

"Dickie V" was Peter's and my favorite announcer—Peter loved his energy, exuberance, and his endless, colorful "Dickie V-sims"—"*W*s" (wins), "*L*s" (losses), "Trifectas" (three-point shots), "Diaper Dandies" (talented freshmen), "Shooting the Rock" (shooting the basketball), "Awesome, Baby" (trademark Vitale praise for about anything he likes), and much more. A lot of times, ESPN would schedule Vitale for the

Purdue-IU game, which would be coming up in a few weeks. I figured the worst they could do was to say no.

So I wrote a letter to ESPN headquarters, explaining Peter's situation, and told them how much he liked Dickie V, and if there was any chance he could say something during the game, that would make Peter's day. I never got an answer to the letter, but at some point we started getting these packages in the mail with Vitale's autographed books, an autographed basketball, and more. Looked like a good sign to me.

The game was during a weeknight in January, but I made sure I went down to the hospital that evening to watch it with Peter. Both teams were nationally ranked and fighting for the Big Ten championship, plus postseason tournament seedings, and the atmosphere around Indiana was electric.

Vitale and Mike Patrick did the game that night, which was in Purdue's Mackey Arena. In the pregame, Patrick commented that Purdue and IU fans hate each other, which when it comes to basketball, was not a huge exaggeration. As the game started, it was close, hard-fought, and a classic Purdue-IU matchup.

About three or four minutes before halftime, Purdue coach Gene Keady pulled his All-American, Glen "Big Dog" Robinson to give him a few minutes extra rest before half, and I could just tell it was coming. I nudged Peter and told him to "check this out."

"While we've got a break in the action, I just want to say a big hi to a great Purdue fan, Peter Boone, who's watching the game from Riley Children's Hospital there in Indianapolis," said Vitale. "You cheer on those Boilers, Peter, keep getting well, and come home soon. You're awesome, baby!"

For once in his life, Peter was at a loss for words, totally caught off guard. I knew that when it sunk in, he would love it, but it was going to take a few minutes before that happened.

Before Vitale's greeting, the nurses, who had also been watching the game, could tell it was coming too and had quietly crowded up to Peter's door. (ESPN had obviously vetted my request with Riley

Hospital to make sure it wasn't some hoax, and the nurses had "insider information"). As soon as Dickie finished, they all cheered.

The game went down to the wire, with Purdue pulling out a thrilling, hard-fought 83–76 overtime victory. It had been a good night. Very, very good. God had answered my prayers through Dickie V.

SI Comes Calling

During this lengthy stretch in the hospital, and with Sandra still recovering from her cancer treatment, it was more than we could handle to spend every weekend with Peter. One weekend my parents were staying with him, and I got a call from my mom. At first I feared something had gone wrong medically, but by her tone, it wasn't that.

"Peter's got something he wants me to tell you," she said. "We were just watching TV, and the phone rang. It was some writer from *Sports Illustrated,* a Rick Reilly, and he wanted to interview Peter for an upcoming story."

What?

A few weeks later, the March 7, 1994, issue had a feature story by Reilly, one of *SI's* best writers, about Vitale. The theme of the article was how Vitale "had a big mouth, but also had a big heart." The in-depth story detailed how, behind the scenes, Vitale went out of his way to use his considerable platform to try to make life a little brighter for some of his less-fortunate fans.

It was a nice story, and Peter was mentioned twice—once about Vitale rising early to pray for people on his "list"—including "that kid in Indianapolis so he won't have to have another operation." And later in the article, it tells how Reilly had interviewed Peter—who couldn't talk on the phone, but could only "click" to answer questions. In the interview, Reilly had asked Peter, among other things, if Vitale was his favorite broadcaster, to which Peter had clicked an enthusiastic three times!

Peter had loved sports for as long as he could comprehend them, and although he couldn't be an athlete in body, he was a great one in spirit, and had regularly read *Sports Illustrated* ever since he was old enough to read. Actually making it into America's premier sports magazine was more than he could have ever dreamed, and he was thrilled! And he got a lot of positive attention, from both the ESPN mention and the article. He even got a few requests for autographed copies. Acquaintances and friends from other states called or wrote us to say how much they enjoyed it and were glad for Peter.

And as a sports-loving dad, I'd had one son "in the NFL," and now I had another in *Sports Illustrated*. I was very proud. I was also very blessed.

You're Doing *What?*

In March, Peter's long stay in the Riley Hospital Burn Unit was finally drawing to a close, and we were hopeful of a release home soon. I was staying with him there one Saturday.

"Hey Dad." Usually this greeting was a lead-in to something sports related, but this time he seemed more serious than usual.

"I'm going to the prom this year."

Huh? I was speechless, on numerous counts.

He'd asked someone last year, and been turned down. And while I was disappointed for him, I could understand why a lot of girls would elect to not go to their prom with a kid in a wheelchair who couldn't talk, couldn't eat, and didn't drive. Now he's lying here in a hospital bed in the Riley ICU Burn Unit, telling me he *is* going to the prom this year? Obviously last year's experience hadn't provoked any tail-between-his-legs attitude this year. The wheels in my head were still spinning, trying to process this.

"So what's the deal, Pete?"

"I'm taking Erin Blair."

Say what?

He'd told me in the past that this girl at school, Erin, had befriended him, seemed to have taken a genuine interest in him, but I really hadn't thought much about it. But taking Erin Blair to the prom? She had graduated a year ahead of Peter, was already in college at Ball State, and during her time at Southwood had been a cheerleader, and one of the best-looking, most popular girls in school. I remember thinking to myself, *How'd he do that?*

***

Peter finally got released from Riley sometime in March, and at the appointed date in April, the big day came. Proms were much more Sandra's thing than mine, and she was so happy and excited for Peter that her prom planning went into overdrive. And she did a great job!

Even though Erin was now a freshman in college and this was not your normal prom situation, it was quickly obvious that she'd brought her "A game" for Peter. When Erin got to our house, she was dressed to kill in a new gown, had her nails done, and had a really elaborate 'do. Most guys take their prom dates out to some fancy restaurant before the prom. But we had a drastically different situation here. So Sandra turned our living room into a "fine restaurant," complete with elegant tablecloth and well-dressed "servers," Tonya and Brad Davis, Rich and Sandy's son.

Sandra had prepared a gourmet meal that included a number of courses, which were served on our best china. I tried not to be obvious, but on those brief glimpses into the living room, Peter and Erin both appeared to be genuinely enjoying themselves and each other in this unique experience.

The rest of us were hanging out in the dining room, which adjoined, and we were joined by Sandra's mom, Rich and Sandy Davis, and John and Jean Myers, friends who lived just a couple of houses away. We were having a party of sorts of our own, just enjoying the goings-on in the next room.

As the meal progressed and servers shuttled back and forth, I remember Rich saying, "This is so much fun; we ought to do this every year."

Just when dinner was over, some "guests" dropped in. Sandra's dad and her brother Randy had left the field during spring planting to be present for this occasion. Randy started doing what amounted to a comedy routine where he acted like a dim-witted farmer and told corny jokes. Peter loved it, but I remember wondering what Erin thought of this. Whatever her feelings, she took this dubious "entertainment" in stride, and seemed to actually be enjoying it.

"I really did. I have uncles who act kind of like that," she said later. "It made me feel right at home."

When it was time to head to the prom, we'd had our family's accessible van scrubbed and polished, and Sandra had recruited a "chauffeur," Todd Davis, Rich and Sandy's second son, so that Peter wouldn't have to endure the indignity of having his dad take him to the prom. Todd wore a top hat for the occasion and played his role well.

Once at the prom, Peter and Erin enjoyed it to the max, and spent most of the evening dancing the night away.

"Sometimes he'd move his wheelchair some, but mostly he'd just sit there and move his arms with me," said Erin. "And sometimes I'd hold his hand and dance around his wheelchair. He was an awesome dancer."

I picked Peter and Erin up when the prom was over and brought them back to our house, where they watched a movie and played games till about one thirty in the morning, then we took her home. As Sandra and I got him ready for bed, she noticed that he seemed to feel warmer than normal. She took his temperature, and found that he had 101. But no one would have ever guessed it. Peter was *not* going to let a little thing like a couple odd degrees of fever get in the way of having a good time at his senior prom!

I asked him how it went, and he said "Great," but really didn't say much else about it, and seemed uncharacteristically quiet. But he had this what I would describe as a "very satisfied glow" about him, which I interpreted as him still processing and reliving the evening's events himself, and was just being totally, serenely happy in a way he'd never been before, over something he'd never done before. He'd pulled it off!

***

For as long as I live, I will be grateful beyond words to Erin for giving Peter one of the best days and one of the best memories of his life. As I was writing this book, Erin, now a happily-married mother of four living in Wisconsin, shared the following recollections of that evening with me.

"When I went to see Peter in the hospital, I had no idea this was coming, but I noticed that he seemed kind of nervous. When he asked if I'd mind going to the prom with him, I was like 'Oh wow, Peter, I would love to go with you. Thank you for even asking me; I think this is the best thing ever.' I was honored that he'd asked me, and I never thought twice. Because everybody talked to him, everybody liked him, he was so real, and because Peter was the definition of 'good.' It always seemed to me that people thought of me as 'Todd Blair's little sister' because my brother had been a basketball star. But if Peter thought enough of me to ask me, that must mean I'm okay.

"And it was so much fun! I went to other proms, but today, that's the one my daughters know about. Looking back and knowing the kind of man that Peter became, I'm really glad that I got to do that with him. I was truly blessed to have him as my friend."

Approaching Graduation

Sometime in late March, Peter was able to return to school. In all, he'd missed nearly four months, but near miraculously, we'd been able to piece together enough interventions for him to keep up with his schoolwork, and he was going to reach his goal—he would be graduating with his class! He was delighted and thankful to be back, and both classmates and teachers were glad to have him back. He thoroughly enjoyed those last two months with his friends.

Over the months, word of Peter's incredible ordeal had spread far and wide. And he'd been on so many different prayer chains, which had further made people familiar with his story. As graduation neared, other people told us how excited they were for us and Peter. We had several, who we would have never thought of, saying they were coming just because they wanted to be on hand to see Peter get his diploma. School officials, and Mr. Conrad, the senior class sponsor, worked closely with us and Peter to get everything just right for the big night to come.

***

In the weeks before graduation, Peter received some really nice awards. Although he'd missed the entire high school basketball season while in the hospital, he nevertheless received a second "Most Valuable Person" award at the winter sports athletic banquet. It was from the varsity basketball team, many of whom were his classmates and "teammates" from his junior high and freshman days. They'd dedicated their season to Peter, and presented him with a nice trophy with a mounted basketball, which had been signed by all of the team members and coaches. The trophy was inscribed with the words, "Thanks for being such a great inspiration for us all. You have motivated us to work hard for our goals, to be thankful for our gifts and talents, and to never quit. We love you, Pete."

Although he was not technically an athlete, Peter was very involved in the high school's Fellowship of Christian Athletes chapter. At the annual spring banquet, since he was not an athlete, he received the FCA Member of the Year award.

He received a plaque from the senior class that was inscribed, "Thank you for being an inspiration to all of us."

And at the spring academic awards program, he received a very special surprise award. In announcing the award, Bob Dawes, the guidance director and a very supportive friend to Peter, led off by saying that one thing the soon-to-be-announced award was definitely *not*—"it was certainly *not* for perfect attendance," which cracked Peter up and drew a nice laugh from the crowd.

Mr. Dawes then announced the beginning of the "Peter Boone Mental Attitude Award," of which Peter was the first recipient. The award was a plaque that would remain in the school, and each year for the next twenty-five, would have inscribed the name of each year's recipient. It was inscribed, "Your courage and joy will always be an inspiration to students at Southwood High School." The award was to recognize the graduating senior from each class who had inspired others by overcoming significant obstacles through a positive mental attitude to achieve his or her goals.

***

As the big day, Saturday, May 28, 1994, approached, Sandra was beginning to feel much better, and her excitement over Peter's graduation energized her even further. The "whip was cracking" as she had me and others help get our house in order for Peter's graduation party.

The *Wabash Plain Dealer* came to our house the week before graduation to do a story about Peter's amazing year, and the fact that he was going to achieve his goal and graduate. The writer, Bob Bryan, did a very nice article in which he praised Peter's accomplishments, but also coaxed out of him that he had "suffered from that most common of academic diseases—'senioritis.'"

As school officials had prepared for graduation, they'd never had a student graduate in a wheelchair before. A ramp was constructed from the front of the stage to facilitate Peter's coming and going. For convenience, he was allowed to sit on the stage during the ceremonies along with the valedictorian and salutatorian. He asked if he could offer a prayer of thanks during the ceremonies, and his request was granted. Mr. Conrad read it for him. He received a standing ovation.

Then as the students began to receive their diplomas, the tension began to mount. Prior to that part of the ceremony, school officials had asked the audience to withhold their applause until the end so that everyone could have a dignified ceremony and receive equal recognition. But when Peter's turn came, that request promptly went out the window. He received a second thunderous standing ovation from the entire crowd as he received his diploma and made his way down the ramp to join his classmates seated on the gym floor. And after each of Peter's classmates received their diplomas, they also exited the stage via the ramp as a tribute to Peter.

***

We had expected a big crowd for Peter's graduation party, so Sandra had planned one two-hour time before graduation, and another time after it. And our expectations turned out to be an underestimate. They came early and stayed late. I've been to lots of graduation parties over the years, but neither before nor after have I seen one like Peter's. It was a perfect spring day, and literally hundreds of family, friends, teachers, coaches, classmates, church family, nurses from Methodist Hospital, former White's students from out of state, and many assorted other well-wishers made their way through our home offering their congratulations, commendations, and best wishes, and lingering to enjoy some refreshments.

On one hand, we had so many guests that it was somewhat overwhelming. On the other hand, we were grateful for every single one. I can't begin to remember what all people said to us, but one comment that I do remember came from Ed Schoeff, a Southwood High School teacher and coach.

"I feel like I'm a better person for having known and been around Peter," he said. If I had to give an overall description of what people said to us that day, Ed's words would pretty well sum it.

A verse in the Bible I'd really come to appreciate the importance of during those years was Romans 12:15: *"Rejoice with those who rejoice, and weep with those who weep."* During Peter's darkest and most challenging times, people had literally wept for us. Now it was time to party! And people turned out en masse to rejoice with us, to share and multiply our joy. After all we'd come through to get to that day, for Peter, Sandra, I, and our family, this had been one of the happiest days of our lives.

I'm Okay with That

Somewhere around that time, something new started happening. Peter had been in the paper enough, or on enough prayer chains, or people knew about him from school, or just word of mouth that he was getting to be pretty well-known. I'd go into Walmart or TSC or somewhere in Wabash and pull out my credit card at the checkout. The cashier would see it, and say "Hmm, Boone. Are you by any chance any relation to Peter Boone?" Then I'd tell them that yes, he's my son. It got to be a frequent occurrence.

At first, my reaction was, "Here I am, forty-six years old, and that's the main thing people know me for is just being Peter's dad?"

Then, it became kind of funny.

Then, it became, "If the main thing I'm known for in my life is being Peter's dad, I'm okay with that."

Then it became, "Maybe that's the way it's supposed to be, part of God's plan for my life." And I was okay with that, too.

CHAPTER 17
TALKIN' TRASH

Sports fan that he was, Peter talked lots of sports with lots of people. Much of it was rehashing or anticipating games, or swapping information and opinions. But for a devout Purdue fan like Pete, a good amount of it was talking trash. And he got pretty good at it—both the giving and the taking. But to start, he had to learn some things the hard way.

***

One of the first instances happened when he was in about the fourth grade. One of the teachers, LeeAnn George, a gregarious, fun-loving sort, had made him a bet about the Purdue-IU basketball game

We were pulling into the school parking lot one morning after Purdue had actually gotten beat by that other team to the south, and Peter had lost the bet. I don't know if LeeAnn had anticipated the outcome, but Peter was in possession of a "crying sack" –a brown paper bag with the eyes cut out and lots of great big tears streaming downward. Apparently whoever lost the bet had to wear the crying sack to start the day.

As he got ready to exit the van, I told him it was about time to don the sack.

"I'm not gonna wear that stupid thing," he said resolutely, which was out of character for him. But I thought to myself, a bet's a bet.

"Yes you are," I said, equally determined. "If Mrs. George had lost, she'd wear it, and be a good sport about it. And if you're going to make bets, you need to do the same. So get ready to put on the sack."

Realizing he wasn't going to win this one, we went into the school. As we approached Mrs. George's room, he slowly pulled the sack over his head and drove inside.

As Peter finally did the right thing, the thing I remember is that there were a lot more tears inside the crying sack than outside it. But he'd learned that if you're going to dish it out, you'd better be able to take it.

***

When it was time to head for Indy and make the rounds of doctor appointments, we always enjoyed our visits with Dr. Turner, Pete's neurosurgeon. He was good with kids—funny, always upbeat, and liked Peter.

Somewhere along the line, Peter discovered that Dr. Turner had earned his undergrad degree from the University of Wisconsin. At that time, Purdue was beating Wisconsin's football team with some regularity. But the Boilers owned the Badger basketball team—had actually beaten them something like twenty times in a row.

Whenever we'd see Dr. Turner, Pete would always give him a hard time. With his alma mater's major sport teams not doing well, Dr. Turner finally started saying in some desperation, "Well, we do have a good *hockey* team."

From that point on, Pete showed him no mercy. He'd just lead off with, "Well, how's Wisconsin's *hockey team* doing?"—the unspoken, but readily-understood part being, "since neither one of your real teams is worth a rip."

In January 1991, Rich and Sandy Davis gave us a week of their time share to go to Florida, and Peter wound up in Methodist Hospital for something not horribly serious for Pete. Sandy stayed with him and would give us daily updates.

While in Florida, I'd seen in the paper that Wisconsin—finally—had upset Purdue, at Mackey Arena, no less.

The next day, Sandy told us that when Dr. Turner came in to

do his 7:00 a.m. rounds, Peter was still asleep. Dr. Turner crouched down behind the head of Peter's bed, and Peter awoke to the sounds of someone repeating "Wisconsin," "Wisconsin," …

As much as we needed the break in Florida, I kind of wish we could have been there to see that one. I'd actually begun to feel a little sorry for Dr. Turner.

***

When Clyde Lovellette was inducted into the National Basketball Hall of Fame in 1988, Roger said, "I guess Clyde really was pretty good, huh."

Yep. A six-feet-nine Indiana high school all-star from Terre Haute, he'd gone on to become an All-American at Kansas, where he'd won a national championship, had won a gold medal on the 1952 US Olympic team, and was on NBA championship teams with the Minneapolis Lakers and Boston Celtics.

During his NBA career, Clyde had a reputation as a tough, physical player who'd once broken the great seven-feet-one Wilt Chamberlain's jaw. But God works in mysterious ways, and in 1979, a kinder and gentler Clyde came to tiny White's High School, to teach and to become the Warriors basketball coach.

But by the time he got to White's, he was "just Clyde," our neighbor, friend, and a jolly giant, who mellowed even further after getting right with the Lord. He and wife Judy were our neighbors on White's campus and also attended the Friends Church, and frequently he'd sit in the row in front of our family. He'd often stretch out one of his long arms on the back of the pew, and Pete and I would see one of his awesome championship rings. We'd both be intensely curious about which one this was, so frequently during the prayer, I would crank my neck into position to try to read the inscription on the ring.

For all his professional success, Clyde's passion was the Kansas Jayhawks. In 1994, Purdue—led by Glenn "Big Dog" Robinson—played Kansas in a middle round of the NCAA tourney. In the first half, Robinson singlehandedly destroyed Kansas. The signature play came when he scored by slamming the ball through the basket over seven-feet-two Jayhawks' center Greg Ostertag, knocking him down in the process. At first, Robinson scowled at him on the floor, then laughed, turned, and ran toward the other end of the court.

The next Sunday, Clyde was sitting in front of us, and it was Peter's first time back in church after several months in Riley Hospital. As the piano and organ played before the start of the service, Pete, laughing mischievously, mouthed to me, "Hey Dad. Why don't you ask Clyde how he liked it when the Big Dog slammed over Ostertag?" So I scooted up behind Clyde and relayed Peter's question.

Immediately I knew I'd hit a nerve. The jolly giant didn't look so jolly. I just hoped he wouldn't break my jaw.

Then I detected a faint but somewhat reluctant smile, as he recognized that Peter, of all people, had zinged him good. In church, even. Choosing his words carefully, he said, "You go back there … and tell Peter … that if I didn't love him so much … I'd come back there and smack him."

I leaned back to Peter to deliver Clyde's message. Upon hearing it, he laughed, hard. He clapped his hands. He cried. I was afraid he might fall out of his wheelchair. I think even Clyde enjoyed watching his reaction.

Peter may not have earned a championship ring of his own, or an Olympic medal. But when it came to trading trash with those who had, he had no fear. He had arrived!

An early picture of Peter with Sandra's mother, Beverly Overman. Over the years, we don't know what we would have done without her assistance for both Peter and our family.

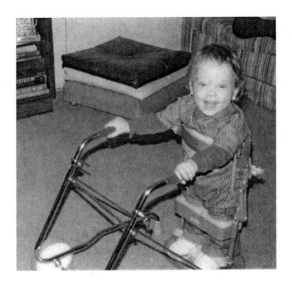

Peter, age two, standing in his "parapodium," with the assistance of his walker.

Sandra's brother Randy asked Peter, age four, to serve as his ring bearer at his wedding to Donna in 1979. Underneath his little tuxedo, Peter has his body brace on, which allowed him to stand. A little later, Peter, with the assistance of his walker, made his way down the aisle to perform his official duties.

Our family at the lodge on White's campus, 1983. Peter, sitting on my lap, is eight, Roger, behind, twelve, and Philip, on Sandra's lap, four.

Peter underwent a spinal decompression surgery at Indianapolis Methodist Hospital in 1984, and wound up in the hospital for three months. Here his Aunt Donna, left, baked a cake to help Peter celebrate his ninth birthday.

"Welcome Home," 1984. Our neighbor at White's, Colleen Spencer, had this sign made and put in front of our house on White's campus to welcome Peter home after his long hospitalization. Philip, also pictured, was glad to finally have his brother home.

"Purdue Pete," 1980s version, stops to hang out with Peter for a few moments prior to the start of the Purdue-Kansas State basketball game in December 1987. Purdue arranged for Peter and me to get courtside seats after hearing of his extremely difficult year.

155

Our family in front of the White House, spring break, 1988. We would have never made it into the White House without an "assist" from Peter.

Peter receiving the best-of-show trophy from the 4-H fair queen for his rabbit "Rambo" at the 1988 Wabash County 4-H Fair.

Peter fishing while on vacation at Lake Wawasee with Dale Pence, background, and his grandpa, Earl Overman. This was one of the rare occasions when Peter actually caught a fish.

Southwood's eighth-grade basketball team won the Wabash County tourney during the 1989–90 season. Peter was the team's statistician, and loved getting to be part of the team.

Peter and Indianapolis Colts wide receiver Bill Brooks at Colts training camp at Anderson University in 1992. Peter's older brother, Roger, was a Colts trainer intern that season.

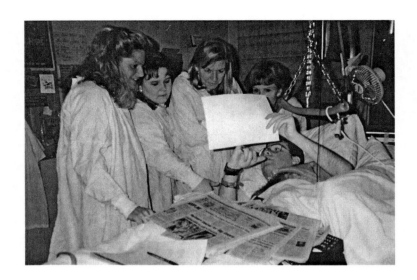

After thoroughly doing his research (see newspapers on the bed) Peter shares his March Madness picks for the college basketball tourney with his nurses in the Burn Unit of Riley Children's Hospital in 1994.

Peter and his good friend Erin Blair at Peter's senior prom in April 1994. Peter had asked Erin to the prom just a few weeks earlier when she had visited him in Riley Hospital ICU.

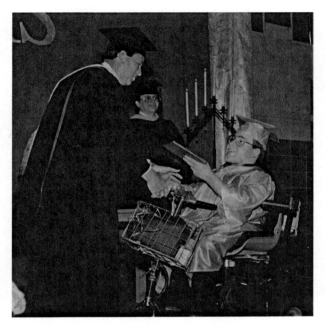

After spending much of his final semester in the hospital, Peter receives his high school diploma May 28, 1994.

Peter in his newly equipped van, complete with hand controls, August, 1995. This picture was from a front page feature in our local newspaper.

Overman family picture in early 2000s inside the Oakwood Hotel at Lake Wawasee. Even though he couldn't participate in water sports, Peter loved going to the lake, which has been a longtime tradition for Sandra's family.

Peter and his cousin Ryan Blackburn before Ryan's wedding to Amy in 1999. Ryan and Peter had always been good friends, and Peter was a groomsman in Ryan's wedding.

Peter, Philip, Roger, and me before the Purdue-Notre Dame football game at Notre Dame in 2000. Boilermaker football and basketball games were a staple of our household.

Peter and gospel recording artist Michael W. Smith after a concert in Fort Wayne in 2003. Peter loved going to concerts, and Michael W. Smith was his favorite.

Roger, Peter, and Philip enjoying a light moment before Philip's wedding to Shelly in 2004.

Going down a zip line at a Joni and Friends Family Retreat. His mother was scared to death, but Peter loved it.

Sandra and Peter at one of the many Family Retreats they attended together. Besides being his mother, she was also his nurse and his caregiver. She did an A+ job in all categories.

Peter and NBA Hall of Famer Clyde Lovellette. Back row, from left, me, Philip, Roger. Clyde was a coach and teacher at White's High School for many years, and was our neighbor on White's campus.

Tim Main, left, was a respite care provider and good friend to Peter, and accompanied him to Joni and Friends Family Retreat as his caregiver there for many years. Here they're in costume as "angry birds," preparing to welcome families to camp, always a festive occasion. Do they look very angry to you?

Peter with former Purdue basketball great Brian Cardinal, left, and his seventh-grade basketball coach Denny Grinstead, behind, in 2013. Peter is wearing Brian's NBA championship ring that he won with the Dallas Mavericks.

Peter had many great nurses during his many hospitalizations, but Rene Cain took care of him at different times for more than twenty years, and they became good friends. Peter recruited her to go to Family Retreat with him as his caregiver in 2014.

"Uncle Peter," with his niece Adeline, and nephews Eli and Randy, October, 2014.

Our family, October, 2014. Front row, Adeline (Philip and Shelly's daughter). Second row, from left, Eli (Philip and Shelly's son), me, Sandra, and Peter. Third row, from left, Randy (Roger and Tonya's son), Shelly, Philip, Tonya, and Roger.

CHAPTER 18
DRIVING

Peter never ceased to amaze me. One morning in his sophomore year, I was unloading him at school, when he popped out with, "Dad, I really need to be getting signed up for driver's ed."

Say what?

Floored, I came up with enough composure to say, "Uh … let's talk about that this evening, Pete. Right now you need to hurry up and get to class."

Driver's ed? How in the world did he think he was going to be able to take driver's education?

On the other hand, there was a part of me that was glad he'd asked. Apparently his friends were signing up, and in typical Peter fashion, this was just one more indication that he saw himself as "pretty normal." He just wanted to do what his friends and any other normal sophomore would want to do. But how do you tell your sixteen-year-old son that he can't just sign up for driver's ed like every other kid his age?

That evening we did have a good talk about it. For all his normal teenage aspirations, he had obviously overlooked a few essential details—like driver's ed cars are cars, not vans; they don't make them in accessible versions, complete with lifts and hand controls; and driver's ed teachers aren't trained for such specialized situations.

When I explained these things to Peter, he understood. But my heart ached for him. I could still clearly recall the excitement and anticipation that I and every other red-blooded sophomore felt at the prospect of being able to start earning a driver's license. Gaining that little piece of paper or plastic that symbolized a degree of accomplishment, freedom, mobility, and independence was a major step toward adulthood and was a fundamental rite of passage.

However, he had got me started thinking about it. Our lives were crazy enough that I really hadn't given it much thought, but felt like I should have. I did know in the back of my mind that it was going to come up someday.

I told Pete that I'd put on my thinking cap and that we'd see what we could figure out. He was content with that for now.

The next time we were in Indianapolis, I made an appointment with Jackie Green, a paraplegic herself, who was a salesperson at Ahnafield's, where we'd had Peter's previous lifts installed. I asked her about what would be involved in getting a secondhand van and equipping it for Peter, maybe with a secondhand lift.

"That's not going to fly," she told me bluntly. "Van modifications are very specifically designed for the individual; they're very expensive, and you're going to have to get Vocational Rehabilitation to fund that. Good used equipment really isn't available, and they don't put new equipment into old vans. Voc Rehab also doesn't get involved until the person is either ready to go to work or to college."

I told Peter what I'd found out. He was disappointed but took it in stride, as he'd learned to do so well, so many times.

***

After Peter graduated, we made an appointment with Voc Rehab, which we found to be a wonderful program, based totally on getting people with disabilities into the workforce. They told us they'd be glad to help Peter "get on wheels," but that we needed to do one thing first—attend driving school. They said they'd pay for him to attend driving school, but we had to come up with the van.

In October of '94, Sandra took Peter to a two-week residential program, Rehab Technology, located in South Bend. It was designed specifically to help individuals with disabilities learn to drive.

To say that Sandra was surprised when the instructor got Peter out driving in South Bend traffic the first day was a considerable understatement.

"When they first said that the students would be driving on US 31, I almost said, 'Are you nuts?'" she recalled.

Peter admitted he was pretty scared the first time, but the instructors apparently knew what they were doing. Soon he was driving in city traffic pretty comfortably. The days were fairly intense, with the students either driving or in class eight hours per day.

"At the end of the day, he was pretty wiped out," said Sandra. "But he was so excited, so proud, so happy. He talked nonstop about when he could get his own van."

Despite Sandra's anxiety over the first days of the program, Peter proudly completed the class satisfactorily and came home with his driver's license.

So we started van shopping. We looked at both mini and full-size vans, but ultimately we selected a full-size van. My brother Gary worked for Ford Motor Company in the Detroit area at the time, and was able to get us a family discount on a full-size one, which saved several thousand dollars.

We actually ordered it through our local dealership, and custom ordered a very basic model that met Voc Rehab's specs. We let Peter pick the color. We were expecting him to come up with some black and gold combination for Purdue, but he surprised us and chose "forest green." We took delivery of it in the spring of 1995. Peter paid for it himself, using the money he was then receiving from SSI.

Before Peter could use it, it had to be modified with a fully automatic lift and hand controls. But he was thrilled! He could see his dream taking shape.

***

We made arrangements with Ahnafield's to do the modifications. There was a few-month waiting list, and then there was an extensive process, which included completely gutting most of the interior, lowering the floor, removing and repositioning seats, and more, before they could even begin to install the accessibility modifications. By the time it would be completed, it would be late August.

When it was finally finished, we took Peter down to get it. One of the owners there, Jeff Ahnafield, talked Sandra and me and Peter through all the ins and outs of Pete's new vehicle, which was pretty high-tech for its time. It had a removable driver's seat, so we could drive it regular style, or could be removed for Peter. A latch-lock system would automatically lock his wheelchair in place to make his chair a "driver's seat." It also had a myriad of other operational and safety features. I'm not sure I'd ever seen Peter more pumped!

But before we turned him loose on the road, I insisted on a refresher course. He'd passed his driving test in South Bend but hadn't driven since October. He had to show me that he was ready. Although he was a little rusty, it came back quickly.

Peter Boone "getting some wheels" was a big deal in our neighborhood and the community. Bob Bryan, who'd done the story about Peter graduating for the *Wabash Plain Dealer*, came out to our house and interviewed him. The *Plain Dealer's* photographer, Harold Chatlosh, got a shot of Peter beaming at the wheel. The article was the lead story on the front page.

Peter's first solo trip was to church. That morning during the announcements, our pastor, Dave Phillips, admonished the congregation to brush up on their defensive driving skills because Peter Boone was now on the road. After the service, many came by the van to look it over, and Peter was only too willing to show it off. Some of the smaller kids wanted to know if they could ride up and down on the automatic lift, and Peter was more than happy to oblige them. Before long, a sign appeared at one of the handicapped parking places, saying, "Reserved for Peter Boone."

Peter was so proud of his new van, and did his very best to be a safe driver, almost to excess. On our country roads, his usual speed was about thirty-five miles per hour. One day I was putting deer alerts on the front bumper, and Roger cracked, "Why are you doing that? Peter doesn't drive fast enough to hit a deer."

But Peter knew his limitations. His motor skills and coordination were okay but not great, and he wanted to leave a good margin for error. Over the years he had a couple of fender benders, but nothing serious.

All of Peter's driving wound up being local. Sandra and I weren't comfortable with him driving long distances or regularly in big city traffic. So Peter drove to work, to Wabash, and around the area. We drove to Indianapolis, West Lafayette, and the "big trips." Peter's being able to drive actually saved Sandra and I a lot of time. And he was very okay with us doing the big trips.

***

By getting his license and his van, Peter, now twenty years old, had crossed another goal off his list. For a young man who was so dependent in so many ways, and had survived so much over the past few years, he had achieved a major milestone in independence. And a huge step toward that normal-ness, to be like the rest of his friends, that he'd yearned for since that spring of his sophomore year. It just took him a little longer. He was so proud. And we were proud of him.

CHAPTER 19

PETER GOES TO COLLEGE (AND MORE)

By the time most kids graduate from high school, they've got some kind of idea where they're headed. But with Peter, neither he nor Sandra and I had really given it much thought—we'd been too busy just trying to survive one crisis after another and get the vexing problem of pressure sores on his back resolved. And, very honestly, we were somewhat surprised that he'd made it this far. Getting him graduated from high school was our overarching goal, and after that, we really didn't know if he'd survive that much longer.

When he graduated, he still had skin grafting that needed to be done, so we didn't get in a real big hurry on future plans. But somewhere along in there, the people from Vocational Rehabilitation had said that with his disabilities, Peter would qualify to receive tuition for college. So we checked it out.

For Peter, going to any kind of traditional college was out of the question. Some Indiana schools, like Ball State, had excellent resources for students with disabilities. But with Peter's situation, realistically the only option was to live at home and attend a commuter college.

As we considered the possibilities, it appeared that Peter's best alternative was Ivy Tech State Community College, which had a branch in Wabash. Frankly, we weren't sure Peter could handle college-level work, but thought we'd give it a try.

As Peter got enrolled, we met Pam Guthrie, who was the head of the Wabash branch. With Peter's marginal academic abilities and the fact he couldn't talk, we had a number of apprehensions about Peter starting college. But Pam, a cheery, positive, upbeat administrator, immediately put Peter and us at ease. She assured us that their staff would do whatever was needed to make Peter's enrollment there have the best possible chance.

He didn't start the fall semester of '94, but waited until the spring semester, which started in January, in order to get his back in better shape. He started out taking a modest load of two or three classes.

On one of the first days of his enrollment, I'd taken him, and was browsing around the bookstore, and wound up feeling badly for him. I was the only one in the store, and compared to most college bookstores, the one at Ivy Tech-Wabash seemed rather sterile to me. We were all familiar with the hustle and bustle of Purdue bookstores on game days, and Roger had gone to Anderson University, and had a great small-college experience, which we'd all enjoyed immensely. But Ivy Tech was different. Despite having some nice sweatshirts in the store, there would be no Ivy Tech football team. No mascot. No homecoming festivities. No real campus, or campus life. Just classes, in a former elementary school building. Peter was not going to be able to have the same type of "real college" experience that Roger had had, that traditional college experience that I was familiar with.

But on the other hand, Ivy Tech was just what Peter needed. He could live at home with Sandra and me, and we could manage his considerable physical and medical needs. He could take classes at a pace he could handle. Our work schedules were flexible enough that we could easily transport him to class. (Peter started Ivy Tech before he'd started driving). We were available to help with whatever challenges might arise. And the Ivy Tech staff was great. They worked well with Peter and us, and seemed glad to have him there.

Academically, Peter did okay, but was never in danger of finishing summa cum laude. At some point, he selected business administration as a major, and computer information technology as a minor. Depending on what was going on medically, he'd take from two to four classes. He had to repeat a couple of classes, squeaked through a few others, and got Bs in some. However in his computer classes, he did well, liked them, and seemed to have a knack for them.

He plugged away faithfully at whatever pace his medical condition and academic abilities would allow. After three and a half years, Peter became a college graduate! He received his associate's degree in the spring of 1998.

Despite my initial impressions about Ivy Tech, it turned out to be a perfect situation for Peter, and I came away with a new appreciation for its mission of helping nontraditional students succeed. The following year, Sandra and I, who up to that time had both been computer illiterate, took the initial computer class at Ivy Tech on Microsoft Office. We both knew that we "needed to join the modern world," and had discovered a place that would help recovering technophobes like us catch up to speed.

Time with Grandpa

During Peter's last year or so at Ivy Tech, he had exhausted the classes he could take at the Wabash location, and needed to attend the Kokomo campus to get the rest of his required classes. This presented a dilemma for Sandra and me. By that time, Peter had been able to drive himself to Wabash, but we weren't comfortable with him driving to Kokomo. And for either of us to take at least a half day to take him forty-five minutes each way to Kokomo and then stay there until he was done wasn't an option.

Then Sandra had an idea. We recruited my dad to be Peter's "transport person." A retired farmer, he said he'd be glad to do that for Peter.

My parents loved Peter and had always been involved in various ways. But my dad was also a very quiet, gentle soul who was a little harder to get to know. So during that period of time, Dad would faithfully show up at our house every week to take Peter to Kokomo, allowing us to maintain our busy work schedules. It was a godsend for us, but much more importantly, allowed Peter and Dad to spend some significant time together and bond in a way that never would have happened otherwise. It was a special time for both of them.

About a year after Peter graduated, Dad was diagnosed with lung cancer, and died in December 1999. We all treasured the time that Peter had been able to spend with Grandpa.

The Return of Chief Running Mouth

Peter had lost his ability to speak in April 1987, and in the years that followed, we'd tried a number of things—adaptive devices—to improve his ability to communicate, but to no avail. We tried one device, but Peter thought it sounded like a duck call, and didn't want anything to do with it. There were also computer devices that could simulate human speech, but again, he didn't like the sound of it, and really didn't want to mess with adding more devices to his already heavy-laden wheelchair.

The thing he preferred to do was to just mouth and gesture what he was saying to others. With his lack of speech, he had also become a master of facial expressions, and that did much to help him get his message across to others. And if that didn't work, he'd write them a note. Obviously not a great system, but it felt more "like me" to Peter, and it at least got him by.

But Dr. Maisel, Peter's gastroenterologist, never gave up the goal of helping Peter be able to regain his speech. Frequently she'd say during one of his checkups, "We've got to figure out a way of getting Peter talking again."

Then sometime in late '94 or early '95, she referred Peter to a Dr. Robin Cotton at Cincinnati Children's Hospital, who she thought might be able to do something to help. By this time, we'd all tried enough things that we were a little skeptical, but wanted to at least check it out. So we added Cincinnati Children's Hospital to our list of frequently visited hospitals.

Over a period of several months, we made numerous trips—four hours each way—to Cincinnati. Initially we never saw Dr. Cotton, but saw his residents instead. It was kind of intriguing. He was this famous doctor, legendary, with a worldwide reputation, but most people there had never seen him. It was kind of mysterious.

Dr. Cotton was an Englishman, educated at Cambridge University in England. At some point he'd come to America, where he became known worldwide for his success in pediatric airway reconstruction. In 1998, he was designated as one of the "Best Doctors in the United States."

As Peter was evaluated, it was felt that there was a reasonable chance that Dr. Cotton could help Peter recover at least some degree of speech. The first step was a series of surgeries to remove some of his salivary glands. Then another to somehow impregnate his vocal cords with Teflon (really). At some point during this process, we actually got to meet the famous Dr. Cotton, and found him to be a gracious and charming gentleman who still had a distinct English accent.

Then the last piece of the puzzle was a device that Dr. Cotton had invented called a stoma stent. It was essentially a silicone "plug" that could be inserted into the hole or stoma in Peter's neck that would allow air to freely pass over his vocal cords, which didn't happen when he had his trach in place. He would need to get his oxygen through a nasal cannula, a tube to his nose, but that seemed a small tradeoff if there was a chance he'd be able to regain his speech.

I forget exactly when the moment of truth came, but it finally did in October 1995. The stoma stent was inserted into Peter's trach opening, and he could make sounds again. On one hand it sounded different than his previous voice, but on the other, it sounded "like Peter." The last time we'd heard him speak was when he was eleven, and now he was twenty, so there was bound to be some difference.

The doctors cautioned us that his vocal cords had been silent for so long that it would take a little "practice" before Peter was talking proficiently again. But Peter had absolutely no problem with that, and "practiced" at every opportunity.

His new voice wasn't totally normal, a little on the rough side, but easily understandable. For Sandra and me, it was a surreal moment. After eight and a half years of silence, Peter could talk again!

***

One of the practices of the Friends Church—also known as Quakers—where we attend is a period of "quiet time" during the service, a period of silent meditation. But it's also a time during which anyone can stand and share a thought, a reflection on the sermon or the Bible, a prayer request, or whatever's on his or her heart.

For the first few days, we'd kept Peter's "miracle" under wraps. But the next Sunday when quiet time came, I stood and said that I had something to be very, very thankful to God for, that I would have never believed possible, but didn't specify what it was. Then I handed the microphone to Peter.

In his new voice, he started talking. To the amazement of everyone in the congregation, he told them about what had happened, how excited he was, how thankful he was to God and Dr. Cotton, and how much he was looking forward to talking with them again, and thanked them for their faithful prayers over the years.

When Peter handed back the microphone, that particular "quiet time" probably became one of the noisiest in the history of Quakerdom, as he received a rousing ovation.

***

So that's how it happened, that after eight and a half long years, Peter started really talking again. And once he did, he enthusiastically did his best to make up for lost time. Just like prior to 1987, we couldn't get him to shut up! But that was okay with us.

That Voice Really Sounds Pretty Good

We were tickled to death to have Peter talking again. But in subsequent follow-up visits, Dr. Cotton felt that with another surgery, we could improve the quality of his voice a little more. We'd always taken the approach of "going for the gold" when it came to trying to give Peter the best quality of life we could, so we readily agreed, and surgery was scheduled at Children's Hospital in Cincinnati.

But this time when he went into surgery, something went horribly wrong, and he stopped breathing. Medical personnel did CPR on him for forty-five minutes before they revived him. Sandra had taken him down there herself this time while I stayed home to work, pretty much expecting a routine surgery. But she called me and told me to get there as fast as possible; she thought this was the end.

I wound up riding down with Sandra's dad, and we both figured that by the time we got there, he'd be gone. But when we got there, he was still alive, although he was having some short-term memory problems.

As the next few days passed, Peter miraculously recovered, including his memory. Whatever went wrong, we never found out. But whatever it was, it scared us, and the rest of his doctors. All things considered, his new voice sounded awfully, awfully good, and there would be no more attempts to improve it. And Peter's doctors and we agreed there would be no more surgeries unless it was absolutely an emergency.

Bad Break

In the fall of '98, after Peter had graduated from Ivy Tech, he hadn't found a job yet, and was just doing some volunteer things and living at home with us. One morning, he lifted his left leg with his hands to cross it with his right leg so he could tie his shoe. Sandra heard a fairly loud pop, and immediately called for me. As we checked it out, when we lifted his leg from the knee, his thigh sagged in the middle. Peter had obviously snapped his femur, brittle from twenty-three years of inactivity.

We quickly changed our plans for the day and rushed him to Riley Hospital. Although it was Riley Hospital for Children, and although Peter was no longer a child, Peter was still followed there by some of his doctors, including his long-time orthopedic doctor, Dr. Lindseth.

When we first got there, Peter was seen by a resident, who had him x-rayed. Sure enough, his femur had a clear break that was obvious to even a layman like me. The resident said that he'd schedule an emergency surgery to deal with it, but before that could get rolling, Dr. Lindseth got word about Peter's being there and the circumstances, and quickly made his way to the exam room.

After one look at the x-ray, Dr. Lindseth said there would be no surgery.

"Peter's had way too many surgeries the way it is, and we can handle this another way," he told us. "I'm going to put him on bed rest for several weeks, and the bones will knit back together on their own. His left leg will be shorter, but it's not like he's a professional athlete or something. For Peter, this is a better way to go."

And as usual, Dr. Lindseth was right. Everything happened just like he said it would, Peter didn't have to endure another surgery, and having one leg a couple of inches shorter was no big deal. Once again, having Dr. Lindseth, who knew Peter from birth, was a godsend.

Mom Goes Back to School

After her year off work following her treatment for cancer, Sandra found herself out of a job. White's had found it necessary to fill her job during her absence, and she was feeling pretty low.

But not surprisingly, she had a lot of Peter in her. She soon picked herself up, dusted herself off, and chose to see this as an opportunity. The spring before we'd got married, she'd received an associate's degree in nursing from what was then Indiana Central College, now the University of Indianapolis, but had always wanted to go back and get her BSN degree.

She enrolled in Indiana Wesleyan University's Adult Professional Studies Program, and started working toward her goal, attending night classes in this innovative program. It was a stressful year for our household, but by then we were pretty used to stress. About a year and a half later, in December 1996, she received her bachelor's degree. We, and everyone who knew her situation, were so proud of her. Peter wasn't the only one in the family capable of turning lemons into lemonade!

Turning the Corner. Sort Of.

To say that the years 1990 to 1995 had been trying would be an epic understatement. While Peter's back looked a grotesque wreck—with the accumulated effects of scoliosis, kyphosis, spinal surgery, and multiple skin grafts clearly evident to those of us who cared for him—he had survived. And his "growth spurt" years were now behind him.

About the time his back was finally beginning to come around, someone introduced us to a new jell mattress that had just come on the market. In our opinion, this did about as much as anything to relieve us of the constant and life-threatening battles with pressure sores.

Even with some tough years behind him, Peter's life and care were never easy. There was always some issue or other with his health—getting the resources we needed; regular doctor appointment trips to a variety of specialists, all two hours away in Indianapolis; occasional minor crises; or any number of other occurrences that were just part of "Peter's package."

But after surviving—for all of us—an extremely tumultuous half dozen years, the next several years were at least a period of relative stability. These years would turn out to be as "normal," relatively speaking, as we could hope for a person about whom little could ever be described as normal. Peter's care was still extensive for us, but as he got older, he was able to pick up more of the responsibility himself. But those years were a very blessed and welcome respite from the routine of constant hospitalizations, surgeries, and crises. They allowed Peter, and us, the opportunity to experience some things that would have been unthinkable during the previous, nonstop crisis years.

CHAPTER 20
CALLED FRIENDS FOR A REASON

For all of our adult lives, our family has attended the Wabash Friends Church. Also known as Quakers, the Friends Church in Indiana is an evangelical Protestant church that takes its name "Friends" from John 15:14, which says, *"You are my friends if you do whatever I command you."* People in our church don't dress like the guy on the Quaker Oats box, nor do we go around using "thee" and "thou" anymore. However, the Friends Church has hung on to some of its heritage pretty tightly— things such as living a simple, Christ-centered life and being a friend and good neighbor to those in need all around them are traditional hallmarks that have endured since the founding of the denomination in England in the mid-1600s.

I didn't grow up in the Friends denomination. Rather, my acquaintance with it followed my interest in this girl named Sandra, who did grow up in another Friends church. A few years after we were married, we went to work for White's Institute—later known as White's Residential and Family Services—which was founded by a Quaker in the mid-1800s as a home and school for orphans and other kids in need of interventions in their lives.

From my earliest involvement, I was struck with how Friends

seemed to me to be very quick to roll up their sleeves, and take seriously Jesus's command to *"love one another, even as I have loved you."* Friends have a tradition of jumping in when something big—such as slavery— needs addressing. Or with something more everyday, like lending a helping hand to their neighbors, whoever that might be.

From Day 1 with Peter, our church family, the people of Wabash Friends Church, had our backs in a thousand different ways. I would estimate that over the years, literally tens of thousands of prayers have been offered up to the Lord on our family's behalf by our church family. Other, more tangible acts of love—meals, cards, handwritten notes, anonymous "love gifts," transporting Peter to some doctor appointments, encouraging words and gestures, and much more—were likewise too numerous to calculate.

But one of the most important ways that our church supported us was in just accepting and loving us and doing whatever was needed to make us feel welcome and a part of life at the church. The concept of accessibility was just beginning to gain some traction when Peter came on the scene, but we always had everything we needed in that realm, even initially, in a nearly century-old building with architectural challenges. Peter was always accepted, loved, and included—just as he was—and very much a part of everything that every other Sunday school kid in the church had access to, even if it took a little extra effort on someone's part.

It all happened naturally, as just a fruit of what people in the church naturally did in loving their neighbors, even before the term "disability ministry" had even been coined.

The following segments tell just a very little of how our church family impacted us on our journey with Peter.

Dave

The Friends Church basically was created in rebellion from the Church of England, which Quaker founders saw as too formal and ritualistic, with too little emphasis on true spiritual development. One of the practices that has come down through the centuries is a continuing emphasis on keeping things informal. While in other denominations the pastor may be known as "Pastor," "Reverend," "Father," or "Doctor," Friends pastors are just called by their first names.

David Phillips, or "Dave," came to Wabash Friends at almost exactly the same time that Peter was born. Dave had just finished his first sermon there the Sunday after Peter's birth. During the sharing time—another example of Friends' informality—a friend of ours from White's, Jerry Garner, had told the small congregation that we'd had a son born the previous Thursday who had some very serious challenges. He asked for prayer for Sandra and me, Roger, and Peter, the first in what would be a never-ending, bumper-to-bumper, superhighway of prayers sent up for us.

From that moment on, Dave joined our journey. A friendly and likable young pastor, Dave was not only our pastor, he became a good friend, confidant, sounding board, hospital visitor, encourager, and much more. During many of Peter's surgeries, Dave was not only there, but was accompanied by his wife, Debbie, who was also a tremendous source of encouragement.

Dave's mostly retired now, but he's still very much a part of our journey.

Susan

One of Susan Dawes's earliest memories of Peter was as a little kid, running his walker into her at the White's cafeteria, just to be ornery. The next real contact she had with him came years later when she was the youth leader at the Friends Church.

"At seventh grade, he was coming into youth group, and I didn't know what I was going to do with a boy in a wheelchair, along with all of the other kids," she said. "But I found out that we could do just about anything we usually did with our youth group. He never caused a problem, never complained; he just went along with the flow, whatever we did."

Susan, whose maiden name was Curless, was the daughter of Bob Curless, who was the former director of White's and originally hired

Sandra and me to work there. She came from a long line of family members who worked with troubled kids. Helping all kinds of people, but especially kids who had drawn the short straw in life, was part of her DNA. While Peter may have done his part to make things in the youth group work smoothly, Susan repeatedly went above and beyond to facilitate the process. And that process included *lots* of concerts.

One time the youth group was at a Petra concert in a nice venue. While she'd ordered a handicapped seat for Peter, the people in front of him were standing up, and he couldn't see a thing. So Susan scouted around for a location where he'd be able to see better, and the only one she could find was in the balcony, which was only accessible by the stairs.

"So I got Roger (Peter's brother) and some of the bigger boys, and we carried his power chair—probably three or four hundred pounds, with Peter in it—up the stairs," she said. "We parked him in the aisle where he could see, but an attendant came up and said he'd have to move because it was against the fire code. I told them, 'I'll move him when you can find me a seat where he can see.' I never heard any more from them, and Peter enjoyed the rest of the concert."

And that wasn't the only time when Peter's accessibility needs were met by unconventional means. "There was another time, at Bobby and D'Ann Stouffer's home, where we were meeting in the basement, and the stairs were steep, but we got him down there, chair and all. Actually, you probably don't want to know all the places we got him into and out of," she said with a laugh.

Susan has no idea how many concerts Peter went to with the youth group, but there were dozens. There were several with Petra, several with Rich Mullins, several with Amy Grant, and even more with Peter's favorite, Michael W. Smith. And somehow when he was with Susan, he frequently wound up getting a backstage pass to meet the artist in person.

And then there was the time in 1989 when the youth group went to New York on a work trip. People didn't believe that she'd try to take Peter on a trip like this, but Sandra went along as his caregiver, and took Peter's van to get him there and around. The group worked at a camp for kids with disabilities just outside New York City. One of the youth group's tasks included resupplying all the fire extinguishers for the whole camp.

"We gave Peter the job of hauling fire extinguishers to their designated locations in his scooter," she said. "I can still picture him, his scooter crammed as full as we could get it with fire extinguishers, running around from place to place. He was having fun."

On that same trip, the kids were having a sharing time, and it was getting pretty emotional. Peter was getting kind of choked up, so he kept having to leave the group to go and suction the secretions from his trach.

"After several such trips, one of the boys in the group told him, 'Peter, we're all sitting here crying and blowing our noses. Just stay here and suck it out right here,'" she recalled. "Also during the night, sometimes the alarm on his ventilator would go off, and the kids would start to go bananas. But they soon figured out that was just a normal part of the package that was Peter, and then they'd quit worrying about it."

Susan not only took Peter places with the youth group. She also occasionally would pinch-hit for Sandra and me by taking him to doctor appointments. She also visited him in the hospital, sometimes taking other kids with her. She said that Peter wasn't the only one who benefitted from being in the youth group.

"The kids always accepted him, would ask where he was if he wasn't there," she recalled. "I remember after that work camp trip, we did some sightseeing in New York City. The kids had to help Peter navigate curbs and other barriers in Harlem, and it made them think about things a little differently. I believe being around someone like Peter helped them to be more sensitive and caring about other people."

Alex

In the fall of 2009, a seminary student came to our church to start a master's degree internship. It was Alex Falder, the once-troubled little kid in Peter's class at Southwood Elementary who had been paddled in gym class for giving another kid a wedgie.

But with his wedgie-delivering days now behind him, a new and improved Alex embarked in earnest on his internship, working with young adults at our church. He had come a long way since those days at Southwood Elementary. Unbeknown to most people at that time, Alex was plagued with undiagnosed attention-deficit/hyperactivity disorder (ADHD). Also unknown at the time, his dad, Larry, was struggling with alcoholism, and the family was in crisis.

But a number of things had transpired in the last twenty-some years. Through the dogged determination of Alex's mother, Linda, she'd sought out and eventually found successful treatment for Alex's ADHD. She'd also transferred him to a Christian school in Marion after his fifth-grade year. And she'd recruited Dave Phillips to spearhead an intervention with Alex's dad, which led to his finally agreeing to get treatment for his addiction.

In college at Taylor University, Alex had come into a supportive and encouraging environment that had further nurtured his emotional and spiritual growth. As things fell into place, a somewhat older and wiser Alex felt the call of God upon his life, and prepared himself for a life of ministry. He started out working with Youth for Christ. Then a Christian camp. Then he served for a few years as a youth pastor in Pittsburgh. Then came grad school at Huntington University, and then an internship at Wabash Friends Church.

When Peter saw who the new intern was, he was excited to see his old friend from Southwood Elementary days. Alex was equally glad to see Peter.

"Peter sought me out early on, and asked if I'd like to just get together and talk sometimes," said Alex. "He actually helped me kind of break the ice in my internship. I figured that everybody among the young adults in the church would know Peter, and he could help me get acquainted with the rest of them."

And so as the two renewed their friendship, Peter would go to talk with Alex on a fairly regular basis.

"I was impressed with how much he'd grown spiritually," said Alex. "As we'd just talk about general things, at some point he'd always ask me, 'How can I pray for you?'"

Sometimes they'd just talk about general things, such as how things were going in each other's lives. But frequently the talks went deeper. One day Alex decided to probe a little more in-depth and tiptoe into asking Peter about his various disabilities. He asked Peter what had been the hardest thing about it all for him.

"I figured he'd have a list of a hundred things of how his physical impairments had impacted his life," said Alex. "But I was shocked at his answer. He told me, 'I've really come to be thankful for these problems. They're what have made me who I am.'"

As Alex's internship began to wind down, various individuals within the church began to suggest that Alex become Dave Phillips's replacement when he retired. Ultimately that's exactly what happened. Alex and Peter had both been born thirty-five years ago, the same year Dave came to Wabash Friends. Dave had ministered successfully and faithfully for those years; the church had grown from about seventy-five to more than five hundred, and now the baton had been passed.

Contrary to conventional wisdom, Dave continued on the church staff in a part-time role. Most times having a successful "old pastor" around would pretty much doom the new guy. But Dave was more than happy to assume a behind-the-scenes role, where he did pastoral visitation and special projects. He was available as needed, but otherwise kept a low profile. It worked very well.

And even though Alex was now the lead pastor, he and Peter continued to "hang out" from time to time. On one occasion, they went to a local nature preserve, Asherwood, where Alex took Peter on a hike through Asherwood's excellent accessible trails.

"I remember his wheelchair ran out of battery when we were at the far end of the trail," recalled Alex. "I had to push him all the way back. That thing was heavy!"

As Peter and Alex continued their renewed friendship, Peter impacted Alex, as he had so many others.

"Because Peter's disabilities were so big, but yet he had such a joyful and thankful attitude toward life, there was something about him that took up a big space in your heart."

Home Happenings

The small groups in our church are known as "Home Happenings," because they typically involve meeting in one of the group members' homes once a month, rotating from member to member each month. There is no "typical" group, with groups ranging all over the place in terms of size, makeup, age, or other factors.

I can't remember exactly when or how Peter became a member of his particular Home Happenings group. But however it came about, from my casual observation, he just didn't seem to fit. Yes, he was good friends with a number of people in the group, but that's where the "logic" in it stopped. All of the other members of this particular group were couples, with Peter being the only single. And they were all older than him—considerably—with literally the youngest of them being old enough to have been his parents. He didn't fit many other demographics of the group either. And Peter, by virtue of being Peter, was pretty much of a "unique package" in his own right. But he loved being a part of the group, and they loved having him be a part.

"I think it was a group where he could feel safe, feel comfortable, accepted, be himself, be an adult, and not have his mom or dad in it," said Susan Dawes, who was a member of the group. "He knew they would do anything to get him in or out of a house, including building a portable ramp for him. But they were glad to do it. He'd just sit around and talk sports with the guys, and he'd talk and share things during the devotional time. I also think that because of all that he'd been through, he was wise beyond his years, which also helped him fit in. Besides not being able to eat, he was just part of it!"

A few years ago, I'd taken Peter to a retirement reception for Bruce Ingraham, who was stepping down as president of a local credit union after a long and very successful career there. Bruce and his wife, Bonnie, were members of our church and also in Peter's Home Happenings group, and would be moving to Tennessee as soon as Bruce retired. Peter and I congratulated Bruce and wished him well; then as we were leaving, Bruce stopped me as Peter headed out.

"Even though we're moving to Tennessee, we want to continue

supporting Peter financially for that disability camp he goes to every summer," he said quietly. "Please let us know when he's going. He's quite a young man, and we really think a lot of him."

A short time after moving to Tennessee, Bruce died unexpectedly. Bonnie continued to support Peter.

Ken Perkins was another member of the group, and once told me about how Peter had impacted his whole family, which in turn had extended well beyond Wabash.

"When our daughter Rachel was in school for speech and hearing therapy, she had a professor who was pretty far out there on a number of issues. At one point, they were talking about kids with disabilities, and he said that 'kids with spina bifida are a drain on society, they can't live a functional life, and they should be aborted.' Rachel came up for air on that one and debated it with him. As the discussion continued, the professor remained unconvinced. To which Rachel answered, 'You obviously don't know Peter Boone.'"

From Served to Servant

As children in churches grow to physical and spiritual maturity, the intent is that they gradually shoulder more of the responsibility of serving in the local church and community. And in this, Peter was no exception. Just like in the other aspects of his life, he saw himself as pretty normal and didn't concern himself with what he couldn't do, but just focused thankfully on what he could.

Every year at our local county 4-H fair, our church sponsors a food booth for fairgoers, with the proceeds going to youth and missions. As soon as Peter was able to drive, he started signing up for every lunchtime slot he could as the booth's cashier, making change for the waiters serving our customers. He loved being at the fair booth, smelling the tenderloins, onion rings, and pork burgers being prepared, and joking around with the other workers.

One time when I was serving as a waiter, I was amused by Peter and a friend, Ryan DuBois, also a waiter that day. They were having a great time ranking the sports teams they "loved to hate most."

Peter also served on our church's day care board for a number of years. But undoubtedly his favorite avenue for church work was serving as an usher. He loved greeting people, passing out bulletins, and helping wherever needed. He also enjoyed talking sports with the other ushers and worshipers, sometimes a little too much. I later became an usher on Peter's team, and occasionally would have to gently remind him to "get back to work."

I remember one Sunday we were taking up the offering. Peter always took the middle aisle, and would rotate his wheelchair back from one section and row of pews to the other as the offering plates worked their way from the front to the back of the sanctuary. On that Sunday, for the offertory they played some song he really liked. I remember him saying, "Oh, man, I love this song." So from the front of the sanctuary to the back, Peter was visibly smiling and singing the words of the song to himself and enjoying himself thoroughly as he served the Lord that morning, totally oblivious and unconcerned with whether anyone was watching him or not. It was fun to watch. I remember seeing one of the older ladies in the congregation, Erma Dawson, nudging her husband Clyde with her elbow and telling him to "Look at Peter." It was cool.

Psalm 100:2 says, "Serve the Lord with gladness; come before his presence with singing," and Peter nailed it. I remember thinking to myself, *A lot more of us could serve so much more effectively if we'd do it with that kind of attitude.*

CHAPTER 21
JONI AND FRIENDS

Over the many years of our annual extended family vacation at Lake Wawasee, we got to know a number of the people who lived in the Oakwood Park neighborhood where we stayed. One year, about the mid-to-late '90s, one of our summer friends said to Peter and Sandra, "Peter, you should have been here last week. There was the most wonderful conference here, for people and families with disabilities, just like you. It was an organization called Joni and Friends. You'd have really enjoyed it."

It sounded enticing enough that Sandra checked it out to learn more about it, and sure enough, it seemed like something that would be ideal for Peter. Her dad, Earl, said that he'd even pay the fee for her and Peter to go the next year. So the two of them got registered for the following year's retreat.

***

Sandra and I had both heard of Joni (pronounced "Johnny") Eareckson Tada, and knew the basics of her story. In 1967, as a seventeen-year-old, she'd dived into a shallow spot in the Chesapeake Bay and had broken her neck, rendering her a quadriplegic, paralyzed from the shoulders down. After an initial period of grief and deep depression during which she contemplated suicide but then lacked the ability to pull it off, she surrendered her unfortunate situation to God, and told him to use her however he could.

190

After a long and difficult period of rehabilitation, Joni, now confined to a wheelchair, started doing inspirational paintings, using brushes held in her teeth, as she used her head and neck to move the brushes. The paintings, which were quite good, became a hit, and both the artwork and Joni received widespread national attention. She published her autobiography in 1976, which became an international bestseller. A movie followed in 1979, and her story mushroomed.

As God continued to work through her, her reputation grew and Joni and Friends was born. Inspired by Joni and her story, a core staff and a group of dedicated volunteers and financial supporters helped Joni develop what would become a multifaceted, international disability ministry. And Joni, who along the way had married Ken Tada, became a powerful voice for individuals and families affected by disability.

She was also an accomplished speaker and writer, and used her unique platform to advocate for the needs of the disabled and their families, speaking across the nation and in other countries. During the administration of President George W. Bush, she served on the Disability Advisory Committee of the US State Department. Joni has also become well-known as a prolific author (forty-eight books), singer, and radio personality. She has received many prestigious awards and honorary degrees.

Joni and Friends Family Retreats are weeklong camps, located at multiple sites around the United States and the world, which serve the needs of individuals and families affected by disability. Through fun, fellowship, workshops, worship, networking, and many other activities, those individuals and families are encouraged to persevere in their efforts by others, many of whom have "walked in their shoes." Families come away encouraged with the knowledge that they are not alone, and that God and others who understand their situations are there for them.

Family Retreat

Summer is a very busy time for me at work, so I was not able to attend the camp. But I helped get Sandra and Peter packed and loaded, and helped them get set up at the beautiful Oakwood Hotel, located on Lake Wawasee, which was located a little over an hour north of where we lived. By the time we got Peter and all his equipment, supplies, oxygen, medicine, etc., loaded, unloaded, set up, and ready to go, it was a very full day. Then I returned home, while Sandra and Peter got ready for their first Family Retreat experience.

"A little bit of heaven" was how Sandra described their first Family Retreat experience. "It was a perfect fit for both Peter and me from day one. There were so many activities and things to do, and the people there were the best part. They were so warm, accepting, loving, and friendly."

There really were activities galore—swimming; boating; tubing; a petting zoo; therapeutic horse riding; workshops; crafts; activities for young siblings, teenagers, young adults, parents, caregivers; and much more. And the whole environment was so positive and encouraging. Participants, both young and old, have the opportunity to share their thoughts and feelings with others who can truly understand what they're going through. Everyone was encouraged to send "Happy Grams"—positive or encouraging notes to other campers.

I was able to come up one evening for "date night," a special evening for just the parents of individuals with disabilities. Couples dressed up and enjoyed a delicious and romantic meal in the hotel's picturesque dining room overlooking the lake. Following the date night activities, I went with Sandra and Peter to the evening worship service. A band played contemporary Christian music, which Peter really got into. But the highlight of the evening was the message, which was delivered by Joni herself, who was present for part of the retreat.

I don't remember the exact gist of her talk, but it was about how some vandals had burned down her dad's classic barn, of which he was very proud. However, rather than becoming bitter or angry, his first response was something along the lines of, "Well the foundation's still good. We can rebuild on this." She then went on to develop the spiritual applications of the story. While I don't remember the "moral of the story," I do remember that it was one of the most positive, encouraging messages I'd ever heard.

Actually seeing Joni in person was quite an experience in itself. Being somewhat familiar with her story, she had kind of become "frozen in time" for me as "that seventeen-year-old girl who broke her neck." Although she was immediately recognizable, it was quite a surprise for me to realize that she was basically my age—graying hair and all!

But it was also evident that she'd grown in grace during all of those years. Rather than someone who was just "confined to a wheelchair," her entire presence radiated joy, happiness, warmth, good humor, and peace, all wrapped in a servant's heart. She was an incredible object lesson, personified, in the amazing abundance of fruit that God can produce in a person—even a horribly damaged one—who puts himself or herself fully into his hands. Who better to develop a ministry that hit an absolute bulls-eye in serving the unique needs of people affected by disability, including our son?

What Limits?

After the first year—actually, more like the first day—Peter and Sandra were hooked on Family Retreat, also known as "camp." And after the first year, Peter quickly identified Family Retreat as a ministry where he could not only have the time of his life, but one with which he could personally identify, and use as an opportunity to serve others who were similarly impacted by a variety of challenges. So after the first year, he volunteered to become a "short-term missionary" or "STM" and serve in a leadership capacity. He started as an assistant leader for teens, and then later with young adults.

But now that he was a leader didn't mean he couldn't still fully enjoy all of the activities and everything else that was part of the retreat. One of the hallmarks of camp is the attitude that here, the line between those with disabilities and those supposedly "normal" individuals pretty much disappears for the week. There are enough people there with various challenges that what is abnormal pretty much becomes the norm, and for that week the playing field is pretty level. All, especially those with disabilities, are encouraged to think positively and push the limits of what they can do.

Sometime during those early years, a climbing wall and a zip line were added to the activities at Oakwood. One day someone told Sandra that Amos Gross, a friend of Peter's who was born with a seriously misshapen and undersized lower body and got around by using his hands and arms to propel himself on a skateboard, was trying to talk Peter into going down the zip line.

"There's no way Peter would do that; that would be absolutely crazy," she replied. "He has no use of his lower body, he's on oxygen, has a suction machine, a tracheostomy, and, well, I just know he'd never be silly enough to even think about that."

But apparently Amos got him talked into it (which probably wasn't all that hard) and Peter likely figured it would be easier to get forgiveness from Mom than permission from her. The next thing she knew, someone told her that not only was Peter going to go down the zip line, but that the staff were getting him into position for his ride.

"I couldn't bear to watch," she recalled. "So I just went to our room and prayed the whole time. I told God, 'Please protect him. But if you decide to take him while he's doing this, at least I know he was doing something he loved.'"

A short time later, she encountered Peter, who had ditched his oxygen and suction machine for the brief duration of the slide, and was now beaming from ear to ear. "It was awesome!" he exclaimed.

***

After the first year or two, Sandra was so enthusiastic about Family Retreat and what it did for those with disabilities and their families that she recruited friends and church family to get involved whenever she got the chance. Over the years, she was able to get many individuals to help, visit, or contribute in some way or other.

One couple that participated in a really cool way for years was Jerry and Barb Garner. They lived next door to us for years at White's, were members of our church, and had a real passion for things equine, particularly draft ponies. For years, they would bring a team of their draft ponies, first to Oakwood, and later Muskegon. Jerry was good with his hands and had invented a small wagon with a handicapped lift on it. They'd take campers on rides around the grounds in the wagon, which was a huge hit!

***

Joni and Ken didn't make it to camp every year, but another time during those early years at Oakwood, the two of them dropped in to spend a couple of days. But they had to leave early because Joni was scheduled to speak somewhere in Europe to a large conference that included several thousand pastors. They needed to get to the airport in Fort Wayne, and asked if anyone with an accessible van would be able to take them there. So Sandra volunteered Peter's van for the trip!

"It was really interesting," she said. "I just let Ken drive, and I was touched by how loving he was with Joni. He gently lifted her into the front seat, and for as famous as they are, they just seemed so nice, so normal. And they both were so appreciative."

And although Joni had been very outgoing and interactive there at Oakwood, Sandra thought Joni looked rather tired and told her not to feel like she had to talk, but just relax if she wanted. She just said "thanks," and appeared glad for the opportunity to rest a bit.

"I really got the feeling that her schedule was much harder for her than you'd think just to watch her at camp," Sandra said.

As time has passed, Joni has not only had her quadriplegia issues, but has dealt (successfully) with breast cancer, and has revealed that she now also fights chronic pain. These conditions have largely curtailed her appearances at the various Family Retreats, but she and Ken still do a welcome video every year.

"It's always great, funny, upbeat, encouraging, a good way to start camp," says Sandra. "Everyone always looks forward to it."

Growing Spiritually

After the first year, Peter and Sandra knew that Joni and Friends Family Retreat would become a must-do annual event. Both, but especially Peter, looked forward to it the whole year. Family members and individuals from our church family helped him underwrite the cost.

A few years into camp, Oakwood fell on hard times and actually closed down for a few years. The Retreat was moved to Maranatha Bible and Missionary Conference Center on Lake Michigan, near Muskegon, Michigan. Oakwood had always been a wonderful and beautiful venue for the camp, but hard as it was to believe, Maranatha was an even better site. The facilities were beautiful, spacious, and extremely accessible, and Peter and Sandra even got to have their own apartment, complete with hospital bed.

Peter loved camp so much that when it expanded from one week to two, to accommodate the many people impacted by disability who wanted to attend, he quickly volunteered to serve both weeks. Every year after the first, Sandra would recruit someone else to go along, to either serve as a caregiver for Peter, or to assist her in doing so, while she served as the camp's nurse. Among those who assisted over the years were Sandra's sisters, Brenda and Rhonda, Peter's respite care provider and friend Tim Main, and Peter's cousin Laura. Tim went with Peter to camp for nine years, and described it as "a blast."

"Peter loved camp, and it was just so much fun just to watch him smile so much, and to be so happy," he recalled. "He enjoyed every single aspect of camp, and didn't want to miss a thing. He wanted to get everything done that he could in the apartment and take along extra supplies so he didn't have to go back and miss out on *anything*."

Then one year, Peter recruited his longtime nurse friend, Rene Cain, to be his caregiver. She said that the experience allowed her to see another side of him.

"He'd always talked about camp so much, and the different people there, but I was never really able to really understand it until I saw him there as a part of it, serving. It was a 'Wow!' and I gained a much better feel for it and why serving there was so important to him," she said.

Rene also had another observation at camp.

"I also noticed that even at camp, girls frequently just gathered around him," she said. "I knew that he had a way with nurses, but I thought to myself, *Okay, I guess this happens everywhere*."

Then, in 2014, Phil and Shelly and their two kids, Eli and Adeline, went to serve with Peter for the first time. Shelly was his caregiver, and Phil served as an STM. They too quickly became hooked.

Shelly recalled that one night Phil was putting their kids to bed, and she was helping Peter get his night meds ready.

"Peter started to talk, and I could tell by the tone of his voice that he was being serious about something," she said.

"I literally, *literally,* can't tell you how much it means for my brother and his family to be here serving with me," he said, with tears in his eyes, of his one-time squirrelly little brother, now thirty-five and there with his wife and children.

Eli had a somewhat different but equally heartfelt perspective.

"Being at camp with Uncle Peter was my best vacation ever, even better than going to Disney World," said Eli.

***

For Peter, camp was a catalyst for a quantum leap in his spiritual growth. Every year the camp had a theme, ones such as "A Mighty Fortress," "Under Construction," "Pressing On," or "Hope Overflowing," each with its own scripture reference. Each camper got a T-shirt every year with a graphic of the theme on it, and Peter proudly wore his shirt every chance he got, both at camp and after returning home. Some of the scripture verses that tied in with the various themes became his personal favorites. Philippians 4:13, "I can do all things through Him that strengthens me," and Philippians 3:14, "I press on toward the goal to win the prize for which God has called me heavenward in Christ Jesus," became two of his signature verses.

"Worship was probably his favorite thing to do at camp," said Sandra. "He loved the music, singing, the fellowship, the sharing, the sweet spirit in the group—everything about it."

For STMs, the schedule was grueling. Peter never had great stamina, but at camp STMs had to be at a meeting at seven thirty in the morning, and were usually very busy until after ten at night, with at least an additional hour and a half required on each end of that for his personal care. The length of the days exceeded his normal days at home by a wide margin. But rather than being worn down by the demanding schedule, he was actually energized by it—helping with leadership tasks, participating in the activities, and, of course, talking. He'd talk with anyone and everyone, especially about sports. Every year after camp, he'd come home with sports memorabilia he'd received at camp—a football autographed by Nebraska's coach, a Chicago Cubs cap, and more.

Out of these conversations grew deep friendships. Many regulars at camp became some of his closest friends, and he touched base with them often. When he was sick or in the hospital, after family, he'd notify his "Joni friends" immediately after, and they were faithful to pray for and encourage him.

Over the years, Peter worked closely with many different Joni and Friends staff members and STM leaders. Two who he probably worked most with were Pete and Carol Taglia, from the greater Chicago area.

"When I first started working with young adults with Peter, I was just an STM, and he was getting started as a leader," recalled Carol. "And I was amazed because he was the first person I knew of with a disability to actually be leading. He had such a heart for giving back, and wanted to make things good for others. I thought to myself, *Wow, this is awesome!* That made me love him from the start."

The next year, Carol moved into a leadership position with Peter, and she was pretty nervous about it. But Peter helped her get off to a good start. And she observed him quickly growing in his leadership role, increasingly taking more responsibility.

"He was doing the devotional time, the schedules, and was totally in charge of all the spiritual dimension, while I mainly did the crafts," she said. "He was there for me and had my back. He was also a prayer warrior. If you don't have that covered, it's not going to work, and he had that covered like you wouldn't believe. He'd become the backbone of our team."

A year later, Peter and Carol were joined by her husband, Pete, on the young adult leadership team.

"We'd kid around about 'Pete and Re-Pete,' and how I was a rose between two thorns," she laughed. "We all got along great and had a lot of fun."

Carol said that even though Peter was a leader, he still enjoyed joining with the other campers in their activities, including playing some of what she called their "silly games." But by doing so, it gave him even more stature with the other campers.

"Peter was really inspirational," she said. "When he was speaking you could hear a pin drop—even with the autistic campers, who are usually noisy and have a hard time focusing. They really connected with him and showed him respect that not everybody earned. Everybody loved him. He was my hero!"

At camp, Peter was on a high all week. Then when everyone left on Friday, he'd crash. Sandra would let him sleep in as long as possible on Saturday, but toward late afternoon, she'd have to wake him up to go to the first STM meeting for week number two. Then he was off and going again for the second week.

At home, he started taking his devotional life much more seriously, and regularly read books on spiritual growth. He'd encourage others, especially through social media, every chance he got, often including some of his favorite verses.

And he'd start counting the days until next year's camp, and begin praying and planning for it.

All of this was possible because a seventeen-year-old girl named Joni let the Lord use her brokenness to open doors of understanding and help for others with disabilities. Her example and efforts helped Peter to do a measure of the same.

CHAPTER 22
SOUTHWOOD STAFF

In many areas of Peter's life, we pretty much just took things one day at a time. For one thing, with Peter, we never knew what the next day would bring, and "long-term planning" wasn't as much on our radar as with Roger and Philip. And also, our lives were crazy enough that we had spent years just trying to survive. We didn't have a lot of time for long-range planning.

In that vein, when Peter received his associate's degree in business from Ivy Tech, we had no idea what he'd do with it. What we did know was that he would not be one of those for whom drawing a disability check and just playing computer games all day, every day, would cut it. Peter was a "people person" and needed a job where he could be interacting with others and doing something meaningful. But exactly what that would look like, none of us really had any idea.

Then in the fall of '98, Peter broke his left femur, which took months to heal. Long story short, we just kind of had faith that something would materialize in its time.

Interesting Conversation

As school started in 1998, Sandra went to work at a new job. She had been hired as the new nurse for Southwood Schools, which included the high school and two elementary schools. She'd been selected after only a twenty-minute initial interview, based largely on the fact that from caring for Peter at school for all those years, both she and her medical skills were pretty familiar to the hiring principals. Once on the job, people quickly liked her work ethic and the fresh new ideas she brought to the job.

One day during early summer of '99, I was down at the high school talking with the principal, Tom Mitchell. He started asking me questions about Peter—how his health was these days, how his driving was going, what he was planning to do, and other assorted questions. Then he made a statement that really stuck with me.

"In all my years in education, I've never met anyone like Peter; he really stands out from the crowd," he said, gently shaking his head. "He's been a real inspiration to me, and he's a very special individual."

A few days later, Peter got a call from Mr. Mitchell, asking him to come down for an interview. When Peter came home, he'd been hired as an ISTEP remediation aide! He would be going to work, in a regular job, at his old high school, which he loved dearly. He was ecstatic!

***

When school started in the fall of '99, Peter was assigned to an area in the library where there were about a half dozen computers, plus his. Students who were having trouble passing the state achievement exam, ISTEP, would be assigned to Peter, where they'd each work on their own individualized program on a computer. Peter's job was to supervise, help as needed, and do the necessary paperwork.

Peter enjoyed his new job immensely, especially the aspect of helping students who were struggling. But as with any job, there were frustrations. Peter's primary one was with students who lacked motivation. For someone who had been hypermotivated his entire life to conquer whatever obstacles life threw in his path, trying to get a handle on why someone would have a lackadaisical attitude toward academic material they needed to pass to graduate was difficult.

But otherwise, it was the perfect job for Peter. He absolutely loved being back at Southwood High School, where he'd had such a great experience. Most of his teachers from those days were still there, he'd visit with them regularly, and he took great pride in being a Southwood staff member. People enjoyed having him there, and made him feel welcome daily. At about two every afternoon, he always found a secretary or school nurse who was happy to help him switch his oxygen tanks.

And with most of his teachers from his high school days still there, there was no shortage of people who had his back in countless ways, just like the days when he was a student. Peter wasn't the strongest disciplinarian, and one day he was covering a study hall and the kids were being too noisy. Pete's old seventh-grade coach, Denny Grinstead, who was walking down the hall, stopped in the room and gave the students "what for," which kept things quieter for some time.

And, of course, during his free time, there was an abundant supply of people to talk sports with. Every day, he'd come home with the latest local, state, and national sports news from a multitude of sources—Mr. Finacle, the athletic director; his old "coaches," Mr. Grinstead and Mr. Wente, and whoever else he could engage with on that particular day.

During his high school years, Peter had been active in the Fellowship of Christian Athletes, and now as a staff member, he attended meetings regularly and helped the leader, Jim Sparks, who became his close friend, in whatever ways he could. Peter also regularly volunteered to sell tickets for athletic events, and help the athletic department in various ways. And, of course, he attended as many athletic events as he could, and was always encouraging Knight athletes.

What may have been most surprising was how good his attendance was. He had a few days where he absolutely couldn't arrange doctor visits on his time off, but other than that, he rarely missed. There were some days when he didn't feel well at all, but even then he rarely called in sick. He would just go ahead and push himself through the day. He was thrilled to have a job, to be helping other kids, at his old high school, with people he loved and who loved him. He was thankful, and took his responsibilities very seriously.

Another source of pride for him was receiving his own paycheck. As an aide, it was pretty modest. But with Medicaid paying nearly all of his medical bills, his expenses were modest too. He could now pay for his own vehicle expenses, insurance, other expenses, and have a little left over. Early on, I explained to him that he was now a taxpayer, including some taken out for Medicaid tax. There was no way he'd ever repay the mountain of expense that his medical care had cost. But now he was in a position to give back a little, and he was pleased to be doing what he could.

Peter became a unique piece of the culture at Southwood High School over the next several years. Hearing him zoom down the hall in his power wheelchair became an everyday sound, and people joked that they needed to look both ways to make sure Peter didn't run over them.

Having his mom either in the building or in one nearby was an added plus. With Peter, there were always little tweaks that his situation or his equipment required. Having a very experienced nurse available to him, as needed, was a huge "fringe benefit." In 2011 Roger moved from working at White's High School to becoming a guidance counselor at Southwood. Having his big brother there to check in with and talk Fantasy Football was another intangible benefit.

Sandra and I also very much picked up the sense that Mr. Mitchell had ulterior motives for wanting Peter on his staff. He'd been inspired by Peter himself, and saw that potential for Peter to continue doing that for another generation of students, and even staff.

Old Friends, New Friends

When Peter first started working at Southwood High School, there were plenty of his old friends around. Over time, that changed. Some retired, some got promoted, some moved on to other teaching or coaching jobs, and so on. But as some of those old friends left, Peter had no trouble making new friends of their replacements. One of those was Jim Sparks, who teaches history.

"I hate to admit this, but the first year I was here, Pete was a little hard for me to understand, so I kind of avoided him," he recalled. "Then one day I saw another staff member talking with him in the library, and he seemed genuinely happy to be talking with Pete. That kind of broke the ice for me, so I started trying to talk to him a little.

Then our conversations quickly moved to sports—college football, college basketball, you name it, he loved it. So we'd talk and talk after that. Since then, I've kicked myself for being hesitant. We could have been friends a whole year sooner."

As the leader of the Southwood Fellowship of Christian Athletes huddle, Jim welcomed Peter's help there.

"Pete was our biggest cheerleader for FCA events," he said. "For our annual 'See You at the Pole' event, some of the kids would complain about having to get up early for a prayer service. Then I'd tell them, 'You know Mr. Boone will be there, so you have no excuses.'"

Jim also just enjoyed having Peter there in the building.

"Once I kidded him, 'You're really annoying because you're always smiling,' but that would just make him smile bigger," he said. "For me, Pete was like a Christmas light—he illuminated; he brightened everyone's day. And if you were having a bad day, here he comes, and he's smiling. It was contagious, and you'd smile back. It was a blessing."

The Ring

When the Southwood Knights started playing football in the early 1960s, the program got off to a very slow start. Then in 1969, Felix Chambers came from my old high school to Southwood, and in a few years turned the program around, earning respectability and winning a few conference championships. When Coach Chambers retired, one of his assistants, Dave Wilhelm, took the program to even greater achievements, leading the Knights to their first-ever state championship appearance in 1991, which they lost. Then in 2002, under head coach Terry Siddall, also a Chambers/Wilhelm assistant and defensive coordinator, the Knights won their first-ever Indiana Class A state championship, on a forty-some-yard, last-second field goal, in a come-from-behind thriller. After forty years, the Knights had climbed a very tall mountain!

Beginning in 1978, one of the building blocks of the Knights' rise to prominence was Ed Schoeff, who served for many years as an assistant coach on the varsity staff. In many ways, Ed reminds me of an offensive lineman—one of those key people who do the hard work that's absolutely essential to success, but never winding up in the spotlight. When Ed's son Josh had played varsity, Ed had stepped back to coach junior high, but was still very much a part of the Knights football program.

Ed had got to know Peter during his high school days when Pete was in his business law class. Although Peter couldn't talk at the time, Peter would communicate with Ed by writing notes, and the two hit it off. They'd talk Purdue sports, and before big Boilermaker football or basketball games would put their respective predictions in two envelopes, and then see who did the best.

After Southwood won the championship at the end of the 2002 season, head coach Terry Siddall told Ed that he would be getting a state championship ring. Then Ed had an idea.

"I've always considered myself to have been very blessed to be a part of the Southwood program," he said. "But even though Peter couldn't play football, he was a key part of the overall Southwood family. He was always there at the games, never complained, and was such a sports nut. He was also a great Christian witness who ministered to me personally. I told Terry I'd like to give my ring to Peter, to show him my appreciation for his attitude and being such a great example to the rest of us."

So that's what he did. From that moment on, Peter rarely ever took the ring off. It was sized too big for his regular ring finger, so he always wore it on the middle finger of his right hand. On at least a couple of occasions, I suggested getting it resized so it would fit the correct finger, but he wasn't interested. Apparently he'd seen pro football players who wore their Super Bowl rings on that finger, and that seemed to him the "cool" way to wear it, even if it did seem a little strange to me. But that was Peter. He'd always worn his watch on his right wrist, just because that's the way he wanted to do it. And if he was comfortable with what he was doing, he never concerned himself with what others thought about it.

Throughout Peter's life, many people had gone out of their way to show Peter various kindnesses. But to give away their championship ring? That very tangible symbol of years of hard work and effort finally paying off in a championship? Ed Schoeff was a better man than I was. I never played on or coached a team that even came close to winning a championship of any kind. I'd have given my left arm to have had one, any kind of championship ring, as would most athletes who take their sport seriously at all. And someone would have to kill me to get it away from me. For Ed to have given his away to Peter, after all the years he'd put in helping the Knights fight their way to respectability, was an extraordinary kindness than I couldn't begin to comprehend.

Ring or no ring, Ed Schoeff is a true champion.

CHAPTER 23
(MOSTLY) GOOD YEARS

With Peter having put the worst of his very medically challenging years behind him for a period, he and Sandra and I were able to move on to something at least somewhat closer to what could be called a "normal" lifestyle. Peter always continued to live with us. His multiple conditions and care were such that any kind of independence or group home living was not an option.

As he lived with us into adulthood, to us, and I think to a lot of others, Peter had something of a "dual status" where he had grown into a man, yet was still something of a boy. Peter always had something of a childlike innocence and a childlike sense of fun. But he was really now an adult. He actually functioned somewhat in both worlds.

For as dependent as he was, Sandra and I took an approach of trying to treat him as much like an adult as we could, but at the same time, still saw him as "our kid." And Peter always seemed pretty okay with that. He knew that he was dependent on us for a lot, had pretty well sized up his situation and regularly expressed his appreciation to us, and it really never seemed to be much of an issue for him.

Expensive "Non-discovery"

Although Peter was able to enjoy what was for him an extended period of "good health," that doesn't mean that it was all smooth sailing. There were always medical situations of some sort that would pop up, including a few hospitalizations of shorter and less serious duration.

Occasionally Peter's system, for whatever reason, would just kind of "plug up," and he'd get really sick. When these situations would occur, we'd always be concerned about the possibility of an intestinal blockage, or his delicate health suddenly "going south" on us. On one such occasion, he wound up in the Methodist Hospital ER. After we got there, one of the on-call doctors ordered a series of scans. Then we waited for results.

I'd been somewhere, and when I got back, Peter was excited and said he had some news for me. Apparently the ER doctor on call was a Dr. Sloan. He and Peter had discovered a mutual interest in sports and had been talking away, and Peter had learned that Dr. Brian Sloan was the son of Utah Jazz coach Jerry Sloan. He had also played basketball at IU, where he'd been on the 1987 national championship team.

After telling me all of the "important" information first, then, in almost by-the-way fashion, he said that Dr. Sloan had told him his test results. He had told Peter that he had some good news and some bad news. The good news was that the tests showed he didn't have an intestinal blockage. The bad news was that he was badly constipated.

"He told me my main problem was that 'I was full of it,'" said Peter and laughed.

"Most of the people who know you could have told you that," I told him, which set him off even more. "We didn't have to come down here, be admitted to the hospital, and run a bunch of tests to find that out!"

Depends on the Nature of the Complaint

My mom once told this story about a conversation with Peter.

"Peter, I don't think I've ever heard you complain," she said to him.

"No, Grandma, and you never will," he replied.

And he didn't. For someone who, compared to the rest of us complainers, conceivably had so much he could've complained about, it just never happened. I've never figured out how that came to be.

There was one notable exception, however. While Peter never griped or whined about his huge assortment of personal physical challenges, sports was a different matter. In that arena, he had no shortage of opinions, and no shortage of things that irritated him no end. As I would help him get ready for bed, I would regularly get an earful about a never-ending assortment of topics.

The refs were terrible; they cost us the game. IU fans. The Colts' draft picks were dumb, and here's why ... IU basketball coach Bobby Knight. If Purdue would've handled it differently, they could have landed that recruit. Wisconsin fans. I can't stand the Patriots or Tom Brady. The coach should have called a draw play instead of a pass because the defense was expecting it. Ohio State fans. Some of my cousins in the Fantasy Football League are trying to get me to make trades that are totally stupid—do they think I was born yesterday? And the list goes on ...

Hey, nobody's perfect. Even Peter.

"The Write Stuff"

In 2004, after thirty years, Sandra and I decided to leave White's. We'd felt God's leading when we came there, and now, we just as clearly felt that same leading on to other things. However it didn't happen overnight, and we'd prepared ourselves to transition out. Sandra had started working as a school nurse for our local school corporation in 1998. And we'd built a new home—totally Peter accessible—on the northwest corner of our farm in 2001.

I'd taken some time to figure out my next move, and after looking at my options carefully, I'd decided to take the plunge as a freelance writer. I'd read a book about "best home businesses," which told about an option as a "freelance copywriter," writing news releases, trade articles, annual reports, newsletters, and more for corporations and organizations. I'd always had a knack for writing; it came easy to me, and I'd done a lot of it at White's. And at White's I'd also met such a person as that doing a special project for White's. I followed up with her, which whetted my appetite even further.

I started out doing some work for an ad agency in Warsaw, which was a good way to break in. Then I got some work from a printing/graphic designer in Peru, doing *Crosspaths*, an innovative, all-community newsletter for First Christian Church there, which is the church I'd grown up in. That led to more work doing school corporation brochures, a fun project that further stretched me. I also had three meditations published by *The Upper Room* devotional. I named my business "The Write Stuff."

However, at some point, the farm boy in me gravitated toward writing in the agricultural and agribusiness areas. First I got picked up as a correspondent for *The Farmer's Exchange*, a weekly farm newspaper. Then editor Tom Bechman of *Indiana Prairie Farmer* gave me a chance as a writer for that publication. Then one of his bosses at Farm Progress Companies, Willie Vogt, asked me if I'd do some advertorials for Monsanto, then DuPont Crop Protection, then John Deere, and others. After that, I picked up Farm Credit Mid-America and POET Biorefining. And each opportunity led to others.

Before too long, I was keeping pretty busy writing for a number of ag publications and agribusinesses. But one thing that worked out very well was what had been described in one of the home-based business books, "the opportunity to wrap your job around your life, instead of your life around your job." White's had been good to work with me about flexing my schedule, but having a "regular" job with Peter had always been an extremely tough balancing act. Sandra had been promoted to head school nurse, with more responsibility, and having the freedom to be my own boss worked out very well for all of Peter's appointments and other care.

Early on, Peter even served as my "IT Department." He was decent at it, and clearly knew more than I did. In the beginning, I just did my assignments on an old laptop and floppy discs, then would use his computer to e-mail work, printing, and other correspondence to my various clients while he was at work. We worked pretty closely on some of these things, and he became familiar with most of my bigger clients. Before long, my business grew out of this arrangement, and I got my own equipment. But he still "consulted" for me with some regularity.

As I got into the ag-related writing, I fell in love with it! I could actually make better money from my agribusiness work, most of which was done right at home. But the thing I enjoyed most was the journalistic stuff, jumping in my pickup and running around the northern Indiana countryside to cover an event or visit some farmer and do stories on some innovative practice he or she was doing. I remember reading my dad's *Indiana Prairie Farmer* as a kid, and now I was writing for it! It was kind of like living a dream. I even dragged home some of the new practices I'd seen to our own farm.

I was never able to really work at my business as hard as I'd have liked, however. I felt I always needed to leave a reasonable margin for time for Peter's care—on which I was averaging about twenty hours a week at that time—including doctor trips, and the "unexpected," which we had pretty much learned to expect. I used to get e-mails from Willie Vogt at 5:00 a.m. or so, and I wished I could be able to get the jump on the day like that. But by the time we'd get Peter off to school, it was often eight thirty before I could get started. But on the other hand, when he was in the hospital, I'd always take my laptop along. I did an awful lot of work while staying with Peter there. Overall, I loved my new work; I was having fun, and it worked very well with our crazy lifestyle.

***

In 2004, we also added a second daughter-in-law to our family, when Philip married Shelly, a former missionary and now an attractive young nurse we'd known from childhood. Philip had come a long way from the ornery, mouthy, little kid who used to agitate his brothers hourly. He'd also gone to Anderson University, had done well in his studies in elementary education, and served as the head manager for the Ravens football team. Somewhere along the way, he had become a caring, thoughtful, and sensitive young man. After graduation he'd landed a job teaching fourth grade at LaFontaine Elementary School within our district soon, and had become a good teacher. We were proud of him.

Sisters-in-Law

For Peter, with all of his medical conditions and physical limitations, getting married and living on his own was never in the cards. He never even had a steady girlfriend. But that didn't mean that he didn't enjoy female companionship, or wouldn't have liked to have had those opportunities. Fortunately, his two sisters-in-law, Tonya and Shelly, were able to fill at least a little bit of that void for Peter.

The girls came into our family through two different paths. Roger met Tonya, who was from Kentucky, at Anderson University. Peter knew Shelly from childhood, and one time had even shown rabbits against her in 4-H. But in both cases, Peter signaled Roger and Philip early on that each girl had met his approval and that "the green flag was out" as far as he was concerned.

"When I first met Peter, it seems like he was in bed a lot, and he couldn't talk in those days," recalled Tonya. "But at the same time, he really seemed 'pretty normal.' He was always smiling, always wanted to chat with me. Very quickly, I had to learn to read his lips, and I always felt bad when I had to ask him to repeat something. But he never got upset; he was so patient. The biggest thing for me was that he made me feel accepted and loved right off the bat, and that he was okay with me dating his brother."

I can't remember exactly when he started doing this, but one year for Christmas, Peter came up with the idea of rather than just giving the girls a gift, he'd give them "an experience." Wabash, population of around eleven thousand, is blessed to have a great quality of life and some unique community resources. One of those is the Honeywell Center with its Ford Theater, which draws a number of big-name entertainers every year. That year, Peter's gift to the girls was dinner and a show, all on him.

To some, this may have seemed a little quirky, taking one's

sisters-in-law on what essentially amounts to a "date," but neither Roger nor Phil seemed unduly threatened by their brother's doing so.

"I loved going on these outings with Peter; it was so fun," said Shelly. "Most of the time when I'd see him, our children were around, but going out to dinner gave me a chance to just be intentional about spending good time with Peter. We always had a great time!"

"He always tried to think of something special for me," said Tonya. "Once he took me to a John Michael Montgomery concert, not because he particularly liked country music, but because he knew I'd enjoy it, and it was fantastic, I loved it! Peter was really something else—he actually had quite a way with the ladies."

Peter's "Christmas gifts" were such a hit that they became an annual event. It didn't necessarily have to coincide with the Christmas season; he'd just let them know that at some point during the coming year, he'd take them to dinner and a concert pretty much of their choice.

One year it wound up being a "double date" of sorts, with Peter taking both girls to a Beach Boys concert. As the son of baby boomers, Peter had heard plenty of the Beach Boys growing up, and really liked them, as do most people. Sandra and I went to this concert too. It was one of the best concerts I'd ever heard at the Ford Theater—sold out, and the house was rockin'.

Afterward I said something about "I'll bet when they sang 'Barbara Ann,' Peter was singing along with that one, wasn't he?"

"Actually he sang along with all of them," the girls said with a laugh.

Also, during the song "Surf City," Peter got an idea. He had someone take a picture of him, Tonya, and Shelly. Then, borrowing a line from the song, he put the picture on Facebook, with the caption, "Here at a Beach Boys concert with my two sisters-in-law. I guess 'Two girls for every guy' really fits here!"

He got more than 150 "likes."

"Uncle Peter"

One of the very good things about having raised our family at White's was the opportunity for all of our boys to experience a lot of things they otherwise couldn't have, including interacting with the other staff kids who lived on the campus. One of those, Lisa Curless Ford, was the daughter of our principal, Lew Curless, and his wife, Joy, and was a good friend to Peter.

She told a story about when her first son, Rob, was born. She let Peter hold him, which he thought was pretty cool. Then he told her, "I'm glad that someone's having babies. When it comes to that, my brothers are worthless."

But Roger and Philip both cashed in their "worthless" status not too long after that. Roger and Tonya had Randy in 2005. Then Philip and Shelly had Eli sixteen months later in 2006, and Adeline in 2010. Peter was now finally "Uncle Peter." He knew he'd never have the opportunity to be a dad, but after a long wait, being an uncle was a role he relished.

And he turned out to be a wonderful uncle. He couldn't do a lot of the things that uncles do, but his patient, good-natured manner made him a huge hit with his nephews and niece, who never even seemed to notice his wheelchair or other medical devices. Peter's room was a virtual museum of sports memorabilia, and the kids loved to explore in there. He good- naturedly tolerated being whacked over the head with a foam rubber "Purdue Pete's hammer," listening to "Hail Purdue" about one hundred times in a row when they'd press the button on some Purdue souvenir doll, or otherwise having his stuff messed with. And he always got a kick out of their little boy and girl escapades—like the night Randy and Eli tried to put our cat, Four Sox, into the dryer "to see if it would make his hair stand up." He'd just laugh, roll his eyes, and shake his head.

Peter had always liked tigers, and he had a couple of nice stuffed tigers that people had given him over the years, and he was really proud of them. He did get upset one time, however, when one of the kids had been riding his tigers like a hobby horse!

As they got a little older, Randy and Eli both followed my excellent example and became Green Bay Packer fans. Both would argue with Peter regularly about the Packers vs. the Colts. And later, Adeline got a kick out of hitching a ride on the back of Uncle Peter's wheelchair.

Other favorite activities with Uncle Peter included watching movies, playing "Go Fish," and just hanging out.

"I always remember how Uncle Peter laughed a lot," said Randy. "It would make me feel good just to be around him when he was laughing."

Laverne

Besides some of the wonderful doctors and nurses we were blessed to work with over the years, there were also others who came into our lives, in less direct, but sometimes equally important, ways. I remember early in Peter's life, when Peter had prescription after prescription filled at our local pharmacy, Linda, our pharmacist, said, "I just wish I could put my arms around all of you, and make things better." She couldn't, of course, but her kind and thoughtful words spoke volumes about how she felt for us in what we were going through, and in her role was doing everything she could for us, and wished she could do more.

And there was Bill, our most recent pharmacist. When we went on a short spring break trip to Ohio's Amish country and forgot several of Peter's essential meds, he worked tirelessly to coordinate a stop-gap measure with another pharmacy there to get us through what would have been a life-threatening situation. And for years, part of Peter's dietary regimen included being on huge amounts of Pedialyte. We'd buy it in bulk, and he'd do everything in his power to get us the very best deal he could since it wasn't covered by Medicaid.

But the lady we probably worked with the longest was named Laverne Peak. Over time, her organization went through a series of name changes, most recently IU Health Home Health Care. We'd order Peter's feedings, feeding bags, and a myriad of other supplies through her company. None of us ever met her, but talked with her about our home health needs for many years.

Laverne always sounded glad to talk with us, asked how Peter was doing, did a great job of taking care of us, and would go above and beyond on a regular basis. Occasionally Peter would have a day off and would look forward to talking with Laverne himself when he could. Despite what would have been a fairly demanding and stressful job, she was always in an upbeat mood, and saw that as part of her job to be an encourager to those customers on the other end of her line who were dealing with difficult health challenges. She'd always wind up our phone conversations by saying "You all have a *wonderful* day, now." And you could tell she meant it. Laverne was a joy to work with. This gracious lady brightened our days and lightened our load.

Mixed Feelings

As Peter continued to defy all expectations on many counts, it was kind of a case of good and bad. While we were thankful to still have him, sometimes the reality set in that when Peter was born, I was twenty-seven, and Sandra was twenty-six. Peter was in his mid-thirties, and we were now both in our sixties, and we'd been at this a good long time now. Sometimes I'd think to myself, *What happens when Peter's sixty, and I'm eighty-seven? Am I still going to be doing this?*

And very honestly, I really didn't want to pass him on to another generation. We knew of no independent living resources capable of meeting Peter's needs. Our kids had expressed a willingness to care for him if anything ever happened to Sandra and me. But I didn't want them to have to assume that responsibility. Although Peter was a joy, I also knew the intense weight of the baggage that came with him, and wouldn't wish that on anyone.

At other times, I would think that once I got a little older, we could do worse than taking care of Peter. When we weren't going through gut-wrenching crises, I really didn't mind that badly. As I'd get him ready for work in the morning, I'd catch up on the local and national news. Then when I'd help him for the hour or so every night to get ready for bed, we'd have a blast watching reruns of *Coach*, which we both loved, or *The Andy Griffith Show*, or football games or basketball games. One of the highlights of Peter's week was at the start of *Sunday Night Football*. He'd wait all week just to hear Faith Hill belt out the opening song before kickoff. It was so much fun just watching him having so much fun!

I'm not interested in a "traditional retirement," and always want to stay active and involved. But I thought it could be fun to slow down a little, have some more time. And maybe Peter and I could slip away to a few more games at Purdue, or the Colts, or Indiana Pacers, and others. There was a part of the thought of "hanging out with Peter in my old age" that had an appeal to it.

Year-end Meltdown

In the late fall of 2012, Peter began having some symptoms that made us think that he was likely having problems with cysts in his brainstem again. We thought we'd see if we could put off seeing Dr. Turner until the holidays, but one day I got a call from the high school. It was Raquel, one of the secretaries, saying that Peter really wasn't feeling good and asked if I could come bring him home.

For Peter, this was totally unprecedented. I'd seen him fight his way through some days when he didn't feel good at all, just because he loved his job and was so thankful to have it. But to ask me to come down and get him? He'd driven to work that day, which meant that the regular driver seat was home in our garage, so I took a card table chair down in my pickup and used it to carefully drive him home.

As soon as we could, we made an appointment with Dr. Turner, who squeezed us in for a late-day appointment. We hadn't seen him in some time, and he looked older, and told us he was going to be retiring soon. He suspected we were correct in our hunches, but after a CT scan showed nothing related to his brainstem, he referred us to Peter's pulmonologist, Dr. Tsangaris.

Dr. Tsangaris ordered some tests, and we were all surprised to find out that Peter had pneumonia! And a bad case of it. Because Dr. Tsangaris was a pediatric pulmonologist, he admitted him to Pediatric ICU at IU/Riley North Hospital, and said he wanted to "get on this aggressively for a few days." Peter was put on a ventilator, 24/7, and received several "vest" treatments—where they'd strap a vest on him that would pulsate very vigorously against his chest to try and knock the congestion in his lungs loose—Peter called it his "daily beating treatments"—plus an intense regimen of IV antibiotics, additional respiratory therapy, and several bronchoscopies. Dr. Tsangaris was very worried about him, and even came in on his weekends off to do a couple of the bronchoscopies.

But Peter wasn't responding. He was weak, but in his better moments he was his usual good-natured self, and enjoyed interacting with and teasing his nurses, but the aggressive treatments weren't touching the pneumonia. Days grew into weeks. This was quickly becoming the most serious hospitalization he'd had in about sixteen years. Dr. Tsangaris and the ICU doctors tried to be positive, but the truth was that his life was in danger. And if he made it through it, we were told that he might be totally vent dependent, and/or lose his ability to talk again, which was terrifying to us.

As people learned of his condition, all Peter's cousins stopped in—some from out of state—to see him. No one was saying it, but all feared this could be the last time. And for the first time in years, we spent Christmas in the hospital again.

But despite his grim condition, Peter still maintained his sense of humor. One of the nurses told us that this construction company that does all of IU North Hospital's building projects puts on a Christmas party for the kids every year, and that along with the other kids in the Peds ICU, Peter would be getting a visit from Santa Claus. He was even supposed to make a list for Santa, and so he asked for an I-Tunes card. Peter and I decided to have a little fun with "Santa." With Peter on the ventilator, I had to do the talking for him.

"Santa, Peter wanted me to ask you about the rumor he'd heard that you were really a Purdue fan. Is there any truth to that?"

"Of course there is," said Santa. "I got my engineering degree from Purdue. How do you think I design all of these toys?"

***

Finally, in early January 2013, he very slowly began to improve. He made progress for a few days, and then we were suddenly notified that he was going to be released. Neither he nor Sandra and I were ready. But in today's insurance world, that's the way it is.

After a super crash course in his care, we brought him home.

Sandra and I were going to be providing the same level of care he'd been getting in the ICU, although a discharge planner was arranging home health care. When we got home, for about the first two weeks, Sandra and I—both of us took time off from our work—worked about eighteen hours per day just trying to bridge the transition from hospital to home. Various people from the church and other friends helped out in many ways—meals, errands, house cleaning, whatever we needed. But even with their help, we were exhausted—physically, mentally, emotionally.

After a couple of weeks, we finally got hooked up with a home health care agency that supplied home nursing care for the next few months. That was a big relief, and allowed Sandra and I to get back to our work and a somewhat more normal life. And Peter gradually began to get better. And much to our relief, he did regain his ability to speak.

He returned to work half days sometime in late March, then full time a few weeks later. And while the home health care had helped us through a difficult time, by the end of the school year, we were ready to move back to providing Peter's care ourselves.

Peter had survived another crisis, his first big one in years. This one had been hard, with some real doubts about whether he'd survive. But true to form, he defied the odds again. But not before bringing back up a lot of the old feelings from years ago. And not without feeling, *Are we starting a different trend here?*

Chick Magnet

Despite his age, Peter still saw Drs. Hannah and Tsangaris, both pediatric doctors, and as a result, they would admit him to the pediatric unit when he needed hospitalization. For as sick as he was, Peter actually didn't feel that bad during this one. He had a great group of nurses, including his old friend, Rene Cain. As I had ample opportunity to observe, the nurses genuinely seemed to enjoy taking care of him, even if he was a thirty-seven-year-old "pediatric patient."

Peter's cousin Rebecca was a nurse at the main Riley Hospital downtown, and at some point during Pete's hospitalization she told us that she'd overheard some pediatric doctors there talking about how they really needed a pediatric ICU bed at Riley North, but that "they had some thirty-seven-year-old patient there, and they were afraid the nurses would go on strike if they tried to move him out."

And then during Peter's extensive follow-up visits back to the doctors' offices at the hospital following his release, Peter would always want to go up to ICU to visit the nurses. Invariably they'd be so glad to see him, come running up give him a big hug and make over him.

I, who was always a shy kid, would stand there watching these goings-on, and again think to myself, *How's he do that?*

"Lucky Man"

Following Peter's hospitalization, he had a lot of follow-up visits in the weeks and months to come. Having the more flexible schedule, I wound up taking him to almost all of those, and as we'd make the two-hour trek to Indianapolis, I'd often listen to country music on the radio, which he claimed not to like. But despite his protests to that end, it was interesting that he would wind up downloading a number of country songs after he'd heard them. When I'd hear him playing them and say, "I thought you said you didn't like country music," he'd just say, "Well *this* one's not too bad."

One night he was in his bathroom getting ready for bed while listening and singing along to "Lucky Man" by Montgomery Gentry. In this cool song, the singer starts out whining about everything that's wrong in his life—from his job, to his town, the weather, his football team losing, and so on. Then he stops to look at what he has to be thankful for, and finds out that it easily outweighs those things in his life that aren't to his liking. The last line of the chorus goes, "Lord knows, I'm a lucky man."

As I watched, I asked Peter, "Pete, do you think you're a 'lucky man?'"

"Yeah, I really do," he said with uncharacteristic seriousness.

CHAPTER 24

2014: COULDN'T BE PROUDER

Over the holidays, Peter wound up having a surgery on the pressure sores that had reoccurred after an absence of many years. We feared a major one, but, thankfully, Peter's surgeon, Dr. Selzer, was able to clean them up with a minimally invasive procedure.

After a few days in the hospital, Peter was ready to return to work when school started back up in January. He seemed to be making good progress.

Nothing Runs Like a Deere

It was the Friday before our schools' spring break, first week of April. Sandra and Peter were at work, and I had taken Peter's van to Fort Wayne for the annual maintenance on his automatic lift. On the way home it was raining hard, and Shelly called me to say to get home as quick as I could because Treaty Creek, across the road from our drive, was rising fast.

That's usually not a big deal. When we'd built our house, it was high on a hill, and only the end of our driveway was subject to flooding, usually about once a year for a couple of hours. But this one was different. After a brutal winter, the ground was still frozen, and the water couldn't penetrate it. So a three-inch rain became a way bigger deal than usual. By the time I got home around noon, it was already impassible, to both the north and south, and still rising. In the thirteen years we'd lived there, we'd only been flooded in a few times for a few hours. But we'd never been flooded out.

I picked up Peter after school, but the creek was still rising. Five o'clock came. Then six o'clock. No change. Sandra, Peter, and I began to get really concerned. Before long it would be getting dark, there was no sign of the floodwaters receding, and it hit us. Peter *had* to get home. At some point, he'd be running out of oxygen. He had to be on his ventilator at night. All of his medicine and supplies, and feeding were there. This was a life-threatening situation, and no place but home would work!

Normally we'd have "gone in the back way," driving on the sod around the edge of our field. But with all the rain, there was no way to drive around there. And I wasn't strong enough to carry him all that way, probably a quarter mile through a soggy field. Then I had an idea.

It sounded totally nuts, but at this point it was looking like our best option. I would get my John Deere utility tractor out of the barn, and see if I could drive it across the field to the sod. Then I'd drive it around to pick up Peter. I'd load him into "the bucket" in front of the loader, and see if we could make it back. If it worked, that would be a great idea. If it went axle deep in mud, well …

As I got it out of the barn, I was praying big time. But as I started across the field, it wasn't sinking into mud. This was the first year I'd gone to a "no-tillage" system in which the soil isn't plowed, and I'd had "cover crops" sown into that field. These were conservation practices I'd learned about from writing about some really good conservation farmers who were doing them. The cover crop, annual rye, had extremely thick, deep roots that gave the soil much more "structure," essentially bound it together much better. As I went across the field to the sod boundary, rather than sinking into mud, the tires barely made an imprint on the soil.

When I got back to Peter's van, Roger was there to help me load him and his equipment into the bucket of the loader. Peter, who was the master of "going with the flow," had this kind of, "well, here's another first" kind of amused look on his face. He good-naturedly posed for pictures before we took off.

Again I prayed as we moved around and across the field as quickly as I could. We finally got in the back door of the barn, came out the front, went down the driveway and around into the garage. I picked him up out of the loader bucket and carried him to his backup wheelchair. Thanks to prayers and cover crops, we'd made it!

As I got him ready for bed that night, he giggled.

"Dad, do you know what? After we were finally done with all of that, it was kind of fun!"

Once in bed, he used his cell to put the whole episode on Facebook, complete with photo.

"Hey, all of you people in Florida or on cruises, look at how I started my spring break! We were flooded out of our drive, and this was the only way I could get home. Can't wait to see what other excitement this week's going to bring!"

He set a new personal record of 164 comments and likes.

Don't Want to Go Back

As soon as school was out, Peter and Sandra headed for Joni and Friends Family Retreat in Michigan. This time, they were joined by Peter's old friend and nurse, Rene Cain. On doctor visits to Riley/IU North Hospital, he had "recruited" her, and after thinking it over, she said she'd love to come. Rene served as Peter's caregiver while Sandra performed camp nurse duties.

When Peter came home after two weeks, he brought the usual enthusiasm and rosy afterglow that only Family Retreat could bring him. But he also brought something else. The pressure sores, which he'd been battling for several months, exploded. It was both shocking and sickening to see the vengeance with which they'd attacked Peter— on his back, his hip, and his right thigh.

Sandra made an appointment for him, and surgery was scheduled for early July. As we traveled from Wabash to Indianapolis, all of us felt the weight of what could be a very crucial surgery. Peter hadn't had a major surgery since Cincinnati in 1996, and we didn't know how he'd tolerate it. And the magnitude of what had burst out with the pressure sores was scary.

To get our minds off of all that, Sandra and I wound up playing a game of "tweeter"—which we'd learned from our grandsons—on the way down. In this game, whoever sees a yellow vehicle first says "tweeter," and the one with the most by the end of the trip wins.

Peter texted to Roger and Phil. "I'm on my way to the hospital for what could be some really serious surgery, and guess what Mom and Dad are doing all the way down here? They're playing 'tweeter.'" (The grandsons loved that).

Once we got there, we started doing all the preliminary things, including the paperwork, part of which consisted of advanced directives. It was time for a serious discussion with Peter.

"Pete, we need to talk," I began. "For you, you've had a pretty good run for about seventeen years or so, from about '95 to 2012. But the pace has picked up some in the last couple of years. If things would go south on us during the surgery, and we need to make a decision on whether or not to resuscitate you, what would you want us to have the doctors do?"

He thought for a few seconds, but by the quickness with which he replied, it was obvious he'd already been thinking on these things.

"You're right," he said. "It has been a pretty good run for that time. But before that, it was pretty rough. I really don't want to go back to those days."

And that was it. He'd given it a lot of thought, knew what he wanted and what he didn't, and was at peace with his decision. If he could continue the good days, great. But if he couldn't, he was confident and at peace with moving on to better things elsewhere.

***

The surgery itself went well, and Peter had tolerated it nicely. But the first time I saw the three surgery sites, I thought I was going to pass out. We knew that the surgery was for the purpose of cleaning out Peter's wounds. But we obviously didn't comprehend how extensive a process that was going to be. The wounds on the side of his hip and the side of his right thigh were particularly shocking. They were like caves. I couldn't believe that Dr. Selzer had gone that deep and not hit bone. On both of those sites, I could literally have taken a roll of standard, one-inch athletic tape, placed it flat in the wound, and it would have laid flush with the rest of his skin.

Peter, who couldn't see the newly cleaned-out wounds, was more upbeat than Sandra and I. But it hit Sandra and me like a tank. After almost thirty-nine years of fighting battles, and seventeen or so years of relatively good times, now our son had huge, gaping holes in his body? I couldn't see how something like these caverns would ever heal up. And once we got home, Peter would need to be on extensive IV antibiotics for several weeks, which Sandra would have to administer.

It had been a long time since we'd had to face these kinds of situations on a regular basis. And now we'd had two of them in two years. The old feelings of "I can't keep doing this" resurfaced. Big time.

Soon after, I was out in our barn, struggling with these things, and wound up sitting on my John Deere utility tractor, just thinking. I really felt like this was more than I could handle. So I just prayed.

"Lord, I don't even know what to say," I began. "But I don't feel like we can do this anymore, and I don't know what to do. I'd really like to see Peter return to the 'good days,' but don't know if that is ever going to happen. I don't want to fight these battles, continuously, for the rest of my life." But then I said, "But if that's what you have for me, I'll do it."

Immediately, I felt an incredible sense of peace. I had no assurance that "everything was going to be okay," or anything like that. But it was in God's hands, and He was in control.

***

One day Dr. Selzer was making his rounds, assisted by some nurses, and Peter asked him when he'd be getting out of the hospital, that school started August 14, and he needed to be getting ready. Both Dr. Selzer and the nurses had a look of "You're kidding, right?"

But Peter was dead serious. He took his job seriously, and didn't want to miss a single day if he could help it. After an awkward pause, Dr. Selzer said, "I think that would be pushing it, Peter." But Peter was determined, and so was Sandra. I had my own doubts because I'd seen the size of the holes in his body. But I'd long since learned to believe in the impossible, when it came to the two of them making things happen that weren't supposed to be realistic.

Peter was released from the hospital in mid-July, still pretty weak from the surgery. We had our doubts about whether we should even take Peter to the lake that year, but Dr. Selzer said it would be okay as long as he was careful and took it easy. We arranged for a hospital bed, and had it set up in the living room of our cottage. Peter spent a lot of time resting there, while receiving his IVs, and other family members would stop in to visit him regularly. And occasionally he'd get up and hang out with everyone else at the beach.

But though he was still very much in recovery mode, when August 14 rolled around, Peter was there for the first day! As the district's nursing supervisor, Sandra usually rotated among all the schools. But she changed her schedule to be at Southwood High School all the time for the first few weeks, so she could administer his IVs there. She'd just come into the library, take Peter over into a corner, and hang the IV on a pole to give it, and then he'd get back to work.

Peter—and Sandra—were used to pulling off what wasn't supposed to be possible. Part of me was surprised, but part of me wasn't.

***

Part of the program for Peter's healing included an ingenious little device known as a "wound vac." IU North's head ostomy/wound nurse, Tanya Clary, fixed Peter up with one of these little machines, which continuously suctions fluid out of the three wounds, and helps them to heal faster. I didn't see how such deep wounds would ever fill in, but Tanya was very encouraging, so we tried it.

Each suction hose was attached to some sealed dressings, which allowed the vacuum part of the device to work. The wound vac was amazing. I got called down to school numerous times when one of the dressings "sprung a leak," setting off the beeper on the wound vac, but most of the time I could troubleshoot the problem successfully. Then, three times each week, I had to take Peter to our local rehab facility to have the wounds redressed. Each time it took a good hour or so, and I was the one with the flexible schedule, and it required someone to lift Peter, so I was elected to take him. I'd lift him out of his chair and onto the table so one of the physical therapists could do their work, and assist with positioning Peter as needed.

This also required that I'd have to take Peter to school myself most days, so I just bit the bullet and did it. It took a reasonable amount of time, but Peter quickly began looking forward to these triweekly visits. His primary PT was a guy named Jason Winegardner, who had once been an athlete at rival Northfield High School in Wabash County. He was also a Chicago Bears fan. Jason and Peter quickly took to each other, arguing about Northfield-Southwood, Colts-Bears, fantasy football, and a wide variety of other sports topics.

When Jason couldn't be there, Joe filled in. And when not Joe, Pete's cousin Zach, who was now a physical therapist at the same facility, covered. And when Jason was there, and the other two weren't busy, they'd all come in and talk fantasy football and other hot sports topics. For me, I was torn between thinking about all the other things I should be doing, and enjoying it myself!

But very slowly, Peter's wounds began to heal. I was astounded! I would have never believed that such deep holes could ever fill in. But every week Jason would measure them, and each week they were slightly less deep than the week before. Once more, Peter was beating the odds, to bounce back from what appeared to be a hopeless situation.

Peter continued to make progress. As the months wore on, two of his wounds filled in enough that he no longer needed the wound vac for those, just the one on his back, which was also coming along nicely.

Tragedy Strikes

In mid-November, northern Indiana was struck with a freak winter storm. Lots of blowing, snow, ice, and frigid temperatures. I'd picked

Peter up from school on Monday, November 17, for his wound vac appointment. Sometime soon after, we got word that there had been a fatal auto accident on State Road 15, just a couple of miles west of our house. A southbound car had hit a patch of ice, gone into a sideways skid, and the driver's side of the car had slid broadside into an oncoming Southwood school bus, killing the driver of the car instantly.

As a school nurse, Sandra had been called to respond immediately. She and other school officials talked with students on the bus, while she looked for any injuries, of which there were none, physically.

Soon, we learned that the driver who had been killed was David Rigney, Peter's old classmate, teammate, and friend. David was a policeman with the North Manchester PD, and had a wife, Stephanie (also a classmate), and two children. Peter was shocked and pretty broken up.

David's death had hit Peter's old seventh-grade basketball coach, Denny Grinstead, very hard too. I'd once heard him refer to David and Peter as "two of his all-time favorite boys." With David gone, Denny, now retired, stopped out at school to talk with Peter, to seek some solace from his longtime younger friend, who he knew would understand his anguish.

On Thursday, I went with Peter to David's funeral in nearby LaFontaine. It was a nice service, and Peter saw a good number of former classmates, teammates, teachers, and friends. After the funeral, Peter didn't say a lot, but I could tell he was really processing things. When he returned to school, he told Roger, "I never thought I'd outlive David Rigney."

The Most Normal of Days

The next morning, Friday, November 21, was a sunny morning, much better weather than earlier in the week. When I took him to school, we got there just a couple of minutes later than normal, and I wound up behind a line of school buses. I had to let Peter out on the east side of the school instead of the south side as I usually did.

"Have a good day, Pete," I said. "I'll see you at three ten for your wound vac appointment." He said, "See ya," and hurried out.

Most days, as soon as Peter was out of the van, I zoomed off to get back to work. But that day I had to wait until the school buses left, so I had a better vantage point than usual. Besides all his regular equipment and wound vac, Peter and his wheelchair were also totally loaded up with medical and bathroom supplies, which he needed to take in. As I sat there and watched, something caught my attention. Despite being loaded down like a pack mule with medical equipment and supplies, he was off, eager and enthusiastic to attack a new day at the job he loved, and with the people he loved, as he hurried into the school, not wanting to be late. This was our son, who had overcome so much, doing it once again. I couldn't have been prouder.

***

A little after two o'clock that afternoon, I was in my office at home working on an assignment, when I got a call from, Lori, one of the Southwood secretaries. She said I needed to come down to the high school, that Peter was having some kind of a breathing problem. My first thought was that Sandra was the nurse on duty there, so why were they calling me? But I got in my pickup and headed down.

When I got there, it was immediately apparent that this was no routine troubleshooting situation. Someone hurried me to the cleared-out classroom where Peter had been supervising a class and had lost consciousness. He was on the floor, shirt off, unconscious and unresponsive, while Roger gave him CPR. Philip was also there, having been called over from Southwood Elementary, a mile down the road.

I'd seen these scenes before, and always before, Peter would eventually blink his eyes, shake his head, and start coming to. That wasn't happening this time. Soon the ambulance arrived, and the paramedics rushed him out and headed for the Wabash County Hospital.

The four of us, Roger, Philip, Sandra, and I, all jumped into Roger's truck, and hurried into town as quickly as we could. I called

Alex, our pastor, on the way. This one had a different feel than the previous situations Peter had had over the years.

As soon as we got there, the emergency room doctor, whom we didn't know, came out and told us that he'd just pronounced Peter dead, saying there was no more that could be done. Soon, the coroner came, then Shelly, Tonya, and Alex. The school superintendent, Dr. Weaver came too, as did Peter's old youth group director, Susan Dawes, and her husband, Brent, and Peter's cousin Zach.

Then, one by one, everyone started to leave. I was the last one out. Peter lay there just looking like he was asleep, like I'd seen him thousands of times before. My ears had heard the doctor's words, but my heart hadn't yet accepted the message. Before, he'd always "woke up" from the many experiences of this type, asked what the score of the game was, and got on with life. As I watched him, my heart was screaming, pleading, "Come on, Peter, wake up! You *always* wake up, Pete. Quit fooling around! Just one more time. *Please!*"

But this time he didn't.

EPILOGUE

Dr. Jim McCann, a physician in our local family practice, and who was a member of Peter's Home Happenings group, told us that the official cause of Peter's death was a coronary thrombosis. In other words, apparently his body had "thrown a clot" that had gone to his heart or lungs and caused his death. Jim said this was likely the result of all of those years sitting in a wheelchair and not having good circulation.

A few days later, Sandra was talking about it with her family physician, Dr. Rose Wenrich, who's in the same practice and also attends our church. Dr. Wenrich's simple, nonmedical assessment struck right at the heart of the matter, but from a different perspective.

"On that day, I think God sent the angels," she told Sandra.

Peter's viewing at the funeral home was on Monday, from 2:00 to 8:00 p.m. Friends came early and stayed late. When we ended, something over one thousand people who had been touched in some way by Peter had come, stood in line for hours to express their sorrow, extend their sympathy and prayers, and make many offers to help in whatever manner. Among the visitors was Pete's friend from Family Retreat, Amos Gross, who came through the line, crouched on his skateboard. They shared memories—funny ones, special ones, poignant ones. Many told how Peter had touched their lives, challenged them to look beyond their own problems to "try to be more like Peter." Dr. Hannah and Dr. Tsangaris each made the two-hour trip up from Indianapolis, unaware that the other was coming.

We had another hour of visitation before Peter's memorial service at our church. Nurses from Riley North Pediatric ICU came. Joni and Friends staff from Chicago came, as did people from Wisconsin,

Baltimore, Atlanta, Kentucky, and other faraway destinations. More than four hundred people packed the church sanctuary plus overflow seating for the memorial service, including many students and staff from Southwood High School. And Peter's cousins from the Oakwood Fantasy Football League and his nephews, Randy and Eli, served as pallbearers.

Peter had always liked eagles, and one of his favorite Bible verses was Isaiah 40:31, which says, "Those who wait on the Lord ... shall mount up with wings like eagles." His friend from Family Retreat, Becky Bullard, played and sang "Wind beneath My Wings" to start the service, followed by a number of Peter's favorite Christian songs. Peter's cousin and close friend Ryan put together a touching video tribute. Dave Phillips and Alex Falder, who between them had been Peter's friends and pastors for his whole life, shared responsibilities for the service, and each did a wonderful job of leading in the celebration of Peter's life. Alex used a football theme for his message, paraphrasing as if coming from Peter, from Philippians 3. He talked about "pressing on to reach the end of the game, and receiving the heavenly prize," another of Peter's favorite verses from Family Retreat. At one point during the service, I caught myself thinking, *If Peter could pull a Tom Sawyer and attend his own funeral, he'd be loving this.* And during a sharing time, many individuals told funny or special memories of their relationship with Peter.

During the preservice visitation, we learned that at the Purdue-Northwestern football game on Saturday, the postgame radio crew had learned of Peter's passing and had paid a touching on-air tribute to him, citing his "winning attitude toward life," and saying he was "everything Purdue could hope for in a fan."

***

Up through the memorial service, Sandra and I had been greatly encouraged by people's touching expressions of love, comfort, and support. As the days passed, we were flooded with cards and letters, doing more of the same. Through many of these, we learned the extent—which was far greater than any of us could have imagined—to which Peter had impacted people through his positive spirit and his encouragement of others through his use of social media.

And we also found comfort in the knowledge that Peter was now in heaven with the Lord. There's a Christian rock song and music video, "Big House," by the group Audio Adrenaline, that's especially popular with kids. The gist of the song is about heaven and how, "In my Father's house, there's a big, big table, with lots and lots of food. And a big, big yard where we can play football." The thought of Peter—now whole and athletic, with no wheelchair, oxygen tanks, or any other medical devices to slow him down—throwing and catching passes, or eating pizza again, was wonderful. And a part of me began to look forward to the day I could be there with him, and play on his team.

But somewhere in my life, I'd learned that before you can celebrate the part of the glass that's half full, first you have to grieve the part that's half empty, and the half-empty part was the problem. The grief was crushing. We'd lost loved ones before, including Sandra's mom and both of my parents. But nothing previously even remotely touched this. To lose a child, but also one who had been intertwined with every facet of our lives, 24/7, for more than thirty-nine years, was a totally different ballgame, and was uncharted territory.

To help get myself through those days I did some journaling, to try to "get it out on paper." In one entry, I noted that in the 1992 film *The Last of the Mohicans*, there was one powerful scene where the evil Huron Indian Magua had subdued a white foe, cut his heart out while it was still beating, and taken a bite out of it. I felt like Magua had cut mine out and taken a huge chomp.

Friends and family continued to surround us with love and support. One old friend from White's, Dan Hobbs, came and mowed our yard one last time. I'd already mowed it for what I thought was the last time, but Dan had professional lawn equipment, and it did look much better when he got done. Dan loved kids, and he loved Peter. He was hurting, and hurting for us, and just wanted to do something, anything. I tried to share how grateful I was.

"I just wanted to do something," he said with tears. "Peter was always a bright spot in my life. Even with all the problems he had, I'd see him at ballgames, and he'd always give me a big smile and a fist bump. Peter Boone was the best man I've ever known."

***

During this time, I had an almost instant change of perspective. For Peter's whole life, Sandra and I had both wrestled mightily with the dilemma of "the boy vs. the burden." While Peter was a great kid and young man, the burden of his care was often truly overwhelming. But suddenly freed of the burden, I could much more clearly "see the forest instead of the trees," and even better appreciate the special individual Peter was. And how, like the blind man in John 9:3, his disabilities had "happened so the works of God might be displayed in him" (NIV).

I also gained a better appreciation for how blessed and fortunate Sandra and I were to have had the honor to have been his parents. Despite all the problems, raising Peter had been a joy, a journey, an adventure. And because of it, God had brought a multitude of wonderful people into our lives to share the journey. Our lives were better and richer because they'd traveled the road with us.

Early in Peter's life, I'd wondered what God had against us, or, at times, if he even cared. From a different perspective, I could now see that what I'd initially thought was the worst thing that had ever happened to us was instead one of the best. Our experience with Peter had become an integral part of who we were, and we were better people for having had the experience. It was humbling to realize that God had chosen us for such a special mission and had been with us through thirty-nine very challenging years. And when we looked back over that time, we could now clearly see that, like in the poem "Footprints," God had been at our side throughout the journey, and during our darkest hours, had carried us.

Not unexpectedly, the holidays were rough, Sandra remarking that she "didn't even feel like putting up a tree this year." Her friend Patty DeVore helped her get it up and decorated. But for me, New Year's Day hit the hardest.

At one point I prayed, while crying profusely, "Lord, I know that Peter can't come back to stay, but there are a lot of really good bowl games on New Year's Day, and you know how much Peter loves those.

I'm sure I know the answer to this before I even ask, but just in case, is there any way we could just have him back for the day, to watch them with us, just one more time?"

I knew the answer to this bizarre request before I even asked. But in my desperation, I felt compelled to pour out the contents of my breaking heart to God anyway. A few minutes later, I was going through some things on the desk in my office, and happened to notice something in the sky approaching our house. As it got closer, it was a large bird with a white head, obviously a bald eagle. Although they'd been returned to Indiana a few years ago, I'd never seen one anywhere in this area, let alone flying low and directly over the end of our house where I happened to be at that moment. I wasn't sure exactly how to interpret it, but I was certain that this was no coincidence. God hadn't granted my request, but He had heard my heartfelt plea, and either he or Peter was letting me know. I've never seen another bald eagle anywhere around here since.

The Dream

Sometime during the holidays, Shelly told about a dream she'd had some time ago about this big black rock. One day the big black rock burst, and water gushed powerfully out of it. Initially she had puzzled over the meaning of the dream. Then it hit her.

"I believe the big black rock was Peter," she said. "Peter means 'rock,' and I think it means now that he's gone, his legacy is going to continue to bear fruit, and lots of it."

And since then, Peter's example and memory have begun to bear fruit. Here are some of the ways.

The symbol of Riley Children's Hospital is a little red wagon. We'd used them a thousand times to haul huge loads of supplies and changes of clothes into the hospital during Peter's many stays. In March, Sandra and I donated a wagon at IU North Hospital, in Peter's memory, with a special license plate on the back, honoring all of the great people there and at all hospitals that had cared for him over the years. Several of our family, friends, and Peter's doctors and nurses attended the ceremony.

About the same time, Sandra had a dream that she was supposed to lead a team of short-term missionaries to Joni and Friends Family Retreat in the summer. This was definitely out of her comfort zone, but she organized a large rummage sale at our church that raised enough to send a team of eighteen individuals—most, but not all from our church—to camp, complete with T-shirts bearing Peter's picture. During the Retreat of 2015 in Muskegon, Michigan, the JAF staff reported that they'd received a lot of very positive comments about certain STMs. After awhile it got to be something of a joke among them—"Let me guess. Could it have been another team member from 'Peter's team?'"

Another team of sixteen members of Peter's Team went for the 2016 Family Retreat. Four families affected by disability were also sponsored.

With Peter's care, I'd never felt the freedom to be gone for any significant length of time. But I'd heard of another JAF ministry, Wheels for the World, which distributes refurbished, donated wheelchairs in poorer countries around the world. We'd donated Peter's backup manual chair to WFTW. I checked it out, and in October 2015, made my first trip as part of a team from the United States with Wheels to the Middle East. I went as a "wheelchair mechanic," to make the needed adjustments to chairs for their new owners.

During Peter's life, we had always had access to good power chairs and supportive services. While there, my heart was broken for the many individuals, especially children, who'd never had any chair. Period. Family members came carrying children, or in some cases adults, to get their first-ever wheelchair. As I talked with some of the families, sometimes through a translator, I shared Peter's story, and why I wanted to be able to do something to help other individuals and families in similar situations. When the translator would tell them Peter's story, family members would immediately lock in on it and were visibly moved, and expressed their thanks profusely.

I've never been prouder to serve anywhere, in any capacity, than as an American Christian, in a predominately Muslim country, fitting wheelchairs for people who desperately needed them. While there, I decided that I wanted to do as many Wheels trips as I could during the rest of my life. I made my second Wheels trip to Poland in 2016, along with longtime church friend and former White's coworker Lew Curless. This time I had the opportunity to share Peter's story to larger groups three times—once in a church in Lublin, and at disability conferences in Radom and Warsaw.

In October 2015, Sandra was asked to be on a panel with Joni Eareckson Tada as they discussed the needs of the disabled and their families at a disability conference at Indiana Wesleyan University.

Peter's passing strongly impacted his younger brother, Philip, who at the time this was being written was named the principal of Southwood Elementary, where all of our boys had attended. He's become very interested in disability ministry, and has taken the Joni and Friends course on that subject, "Beyond Suffering." He's planning to teach classes on working with the disabled, and at some point would like to do something more in the area of helping to start disability ministries in our county.

What other fruit will come from Peter's life? I have no idea, and that's really up to God. But Sandra, I, and others want to use Peter's life and platform to try to do some good whenever we can. And we figure if Jesus could feed five thousand people with leftover scraps, who knows?

***

So why did I write this book? Partly to encourage readers to be good neighbors—to be aware of those around them who are going through the deep waters, and to reach out to offer a hand, a thoughtful gesture, or their prayers, as people did with Peter and us countless times.

But even more than that, I wanted more people to experience the joy, the fun, and the inspiration of knowing Peter. And to learn from him and "have your game elevated," as many of the rest of us did.

Things like:

Don't be unduly concerned about what you can't do; be thankful and enjoy doing what you can. Life is 10 percent what happens to you, and 90 percent what you do about it. Let your challenges make you better. Laugh every chance you get, and do it with gusto. Be comfortable in your own skin, regardless of how many skin grafts you may have had. Nurture your passions, cheer on your favorite team, or whatever you follow. Be a friend, take an interest in others, and encourage them whenever you can. Enjoy your work. Whatever you're doing, try to have fun doing it. Find a cause that's meaningful to you and serve in it joyfully. Give back. Don't be a whiner or a complainer. Take some risks—ask someone to the prom or go down a zip line. Just like Rocky Balboa, when life appears to have you down for the count, it doesn't mean the fight's over. Don't let everyday headaches ruin your day, because life's too short. A spoonful of sugar really does help the medicine go down. Make a positive difference in your little corner of the world. Leave a legacy. And most of all, nurture a right relationship with the God who made you; trust in him, and learn all you can about his plan for your life.

And laugh some more.

ABOUT THE AUTHOR

As a high school student, Darrell Boone didn't care for English, particularly the part about diagramming sentences. But, paradoxically, he enjoyed writing, and it came easy for him. Through high school and college at Purdue University, his ability to write A papers gave a considerable boost to what could have been an otherwise mediocre GPA.

Early in his career, Darrell felt God's leading to White's Institute (now White's Residential and Family Services), a Quaker residential treatment center for troubled kids near Wabash, Indiana. There, he worked in a variety of roles, mostly as a supervisor and staff trainer. But he also had the opportunity to serve as an assistant football coach and junior high basketball coach, which he enjoyed immensely. During his career at White's, he picked up a master's degree in counseling psychology from Ball State University, where several of his professors said they enjoyed reading his papers.

After thirty years, Darrell left White's to start his own home-based freelance writing business. Although he has done work for a number of not-for-profits and has had some of his meditations published by *The Upper Room*, his passion for agriculture (he was a farm kid) led him into agricultural writing. He has been privileged to write for such publications as *The Farmer's Exchange, Indiana Prairie Farmer, and Farm Futures,* and has also done marketing and PR work for some of Indiana's and America's leading agribusinesses.

Darrell married his second-grade sweetheart, Sandra, and they live on a small farm near Wabash. They have two adult sons, Roger and Philip, with wives Tonya and Shelly, and grandkids Randy, Eli, and Adeline. In their free time, they enjoy serving in their church, following their grandkids' activities, attending Purdue athletic events, and working on the farm, assisted by the grandkids.

Darrell still doesn't know how to diagram a sentence properly, and at this point in his life, he doesn't care.

CPSIA information can be obtained
at www.ICGtesting.com
Printed in the USA
LVOW11s0349271017
553988LV00001B/78/P